They Also Speak

They Also Speak

A. C. Kruer

BROADMAN PRESS
Nashville, Tennessee

Unless otherwise indicated, the Scripture quotations are
the author's own translation.

Dewey Decimal Classification: 220.92
Subject heading: BIBLE—BIOGRAPHY

Library of Congress Catalog Card Number: 78-67453
Printed in the United States of America

To my wife, Lucile

and

My daughter, Claudia Sherer,

Missionary to Japan

CONTENTS

FOREWORD

We read in the letter to the Hebrews that Abel, because he brought a more acceptable offering to God than did his brother Cain, "having died, still (even now) speaks" (Heb. 11:4).

Then, after recounting the experiences of a number of individuals who exercised remarkable faith, the author of Hebrews writes that time would not permit him to mention the experiences of a long list of others, whose names and experiences are familiar to Bible readers.

The Scriptures also contain accounts of numerous others who can still convey to us worthwhile messages. However, their experiences and messages may not be quite as familiar to many of us, due to the fact that they have not been mentioned by name.

Although a number of these are mentioned in parables, this does not necessarily mean that they were characters invented for the purpose of illustrating the messages presented in those parables. Their experiences represent actual life experiences, similar to those faced by many individuals who have lived, or are still living. Their use in dramatizing a truth or situation should not therefore hinder us from profiting by what they are made to portray.

Inspiration for presenting the following sketches came while reviewing the experience of that unnamed prophet whom God sent from Judah with a vitally important message for King Jeroboam, the new king of Israel.

The purpose and value of these presentations can be expressed in these challenging words with which the author of Hebrews has summarized that inspiring presentation of those who displayed such great faith in God:

"Wherefore (in the light of the foregoing), having such a tremendous cloud of witnesses [1] placed about us, casting off every burden (every hindering encumbrance) and easily encircling sin (that could obscure from view this great crowd of witnesses), through steadfast endurance [2] let us run the race (keep on going, struggling) lying out there ahead of us, looking toward the Author and Finisher of our faith, Jesus, who in view of (over against) the joy lying ahead of him, endured the cross, looking with scorn upon the shame (of that kind of death), sat down on the right side of the throne of God" (Heb. 12:1-2).

[1] The Greek word used here is the word from which is derived literally our English word *martyr*.

[2] Whereas we currently use the expression "stay in there," the Greek word used means literally "stay under."

Mortal Message

1 Kings 13:26-28

What were the reactions of those who passed by this strange scene, a prophet's body lying in the middle of the road, his beast of burden standing quietly on one side, gazing down at his corpse, his killer, a lion, standing on the other side, neither devouring its prey nor molesting his donkey?

How many of those passersby wondered or tried to learn the meaning of this strange scene? Or did they continue on their way, doing business as usual, perhaps casually telling others, then giving their own version of what had taken place?

Realizing that Israelites who would go up to Jerusalem to worship in the Temple might be lured back into the Kingdom of Judah, King Jeroboam resorted to political strategy, placing golden calves in Dan and Bethel and appointing as priests men of questionable reputation, not members of the priestly tribe of Levi.

God had sent this prophet from Jerusalem to warn Jeroboam of the consequences of his political strategy, the doom of that altar which he had erected and of those illegitimate priests.

To stress the urgency of his mission, God had instructed this prophet to return to Judah immediately after delivering his message, and by another way, not tarrying even for food or drink.

Having delivered his message, the prophet started home. However, he was overtaken by a prophet of Israel who invited him to be his dinner guest. When he declined and gave his reason, that elder prophet persuaded him by claiming to have had a later message from an angel, instructing him to bring him to his house.

During the meal, the host confessed that he had deceived his guest, then prophesied that because of his disregard of God's admonition not to tarry for any reason, on his way home he would be killed by a lion.

To speculate as to why one prophet would deliberately deceive another prophet would be less profitable than centering attention on the significance of this strange scene on the road to Judah.

This man's lifeless body lying there between his beast of burden and his killer is one of those many guideposts which God has placed along life's highway to warn those of us who will pause to heed. It is as vitally valid today as it was for those traveling along that road and actually seeing this strange phenomenon.

His message? Simply this, that *God means what he says:* We disregard his counsel and his warnings at our own peril.

"Why did this have to happen to me?" "How could I know it would happen to me?" "Why didn't somebody warn me?" These are among the questions frequently heard from those who are confronted with difficult problems or situations or are victims of frustrating circumstances with which life is filled. Frequently these circumstances are of their own making, simply because they failed or neglected to stop, look, and listen—until it was too late.

The answer? "Someone *has* warned you, and they are the *many* who have left these guideposts"—guideposts which are as clearly discernable as ignored and which could mean so much if only we would pause and realize: "Something like this could easily happen to me also."

On the other hand, many of us are inclined to shrug off such thoughts carelessly with: "That can't happen to me."

How often it has been said that we learn from experience. However, it would be well to remind ourselves that it is possible to learn from the experiences of *others* as well as from our own—yes, and much less painfully or disastrously.

Woman on a Wall

2 Samuel 20

Following the revolt and death of King David's son, Absalom, a man named Sheba [1] of the tribe of Benjamin went throughout Israel blowing a trumpet and announcing, "We have no part in David . . . every man to his tents, O Israel" (v. 1).

King David dispatched his military leader, Amasa, to round up the fighting men of Judah, but when Amasa failed to return within three days, in order to avoid trouble, David directed Abishai, another of his military leaders, to pursue Sheba with all available fighting men.

Abishai and his brother Joab met Amasa as he was returning to Jerusalem, and Joab, aspiring to become commander in chief of the army, murdered Amasa then pursued Sheba to the city of Abel in the tribe of Benjamin and throwing up a bulwark prepared to besiege the city.

From the top of the city wall came a woman's voice: "Listen! listen! Tell Joab: 'Come here, that I may speak to you.'" And when he came near, she called: "Listen to your maidservant" (v. 17).

What could a lone woman expect to gain by trying to reason with a ruthless fellow who had not hesitated to take the life of a fellow soldier who stood between him and a position which he coveted? Not only had he murdered Amasa but, at the beginning of David's reign, he had also assassinated Abner, another military leader, to King David's chagrin and humiliation (2 Sam. 3:22 ff.).

That this woman spoke, not merely with emotional appeal, but with persuasive force and wisdom is evident from the effect of her words upon Joab. When she spoke, he listened, and on the strength of her promise that the head of Sheba would be thrown over the wall, he promised: " . . . Give up him alone, and I will withdraw from the city" (20:21*b*).

The wise counsel with which this courageous woman succeeded in dissuading a man of Joab's character from wiping out an entire city because of the presence of one ambitious rebel of questionable character is also direly needed in our own day, which in many respects is not greatly different from that in which she lived. It is in fact even more urgently needed because of modern weapons and methods of warfare and because of contemporary practices.

They who deliberately or wantonly disregard the welfare of others could certainly profit by this wise woman's reminder of the heavy toll exacted of innocent people who have had little if indeed anything to do with the circumstances on which they base their grievances, even though their motive may seem justifiable to them, particularly, as in this case, when motivated by selfish ambitions.

Surely this wise, aggressive woman is entitled more than a place of anonymity in history. Her wise counsel also brings into clear focus an Old Testament ordinance frequently subjected to undeserved

13

criticism due to a misinterpretation given it, "life for life, eye for eye . . . " (Ex. 21:23-24). The tendency, clearly illustrated by Joab's intention to besiege Abel, is to go far beyond what has been inflicted upon the injured person or persons in order to seek vengeance.

The Old Testament teaching is not permissive but rather restrictive, limiting the punishment to the guilty party alone and furthermore restricting the punishment to what has been done to the victim, that and nothing more. Jesus has not repudiated nor rejected this but has rather restricted it even further (see Matt. 5:38 ff.).

Joab would have destroyed not only the population of the city of Abel but in a sense the city's reputation as well. This woman on the wall reminded him: "They were accustomed to say in old time, 'Let them but ask counsel at Abel,' and so they settled a matter" (2 Sam. 20:18).

And so she herself has preserved for us that city's reputation through her own display of wisdom, for which the city had been known. But for her, who would be able to learn about this city's reputation?

Who was this remarkable woman who should be permitted to speak in even louder accents than she spoke from that wall so long ago? Her identity, unfortunately, is even more obscure than her directly needed but all-too-frequently unheeded wisdom.

[1] "Man of Belial" (KJV); "worthless fellow" (ASV).

Who Was Neighbor?

Luke 10:25-37

"A certain man was going down from Jerusalem to Jericho."

The manner in which the Lord Jesus introduces this familiar story suggests the possibility that the incident has actually occurred and was not merely an illustration. There has undoubtedly been many holdups along that lonely road, but it is doubtful whether many, if indeed any, of them had resulted as did this one.

Although not identified by name, he who proved to be the real neighbor is undoubtedly better known today than many whose names

14

are mentioned, both in biblical and secular history or literature.

The incident was related in response to a question put to the Master by a pharisaic lawyer: "Teacher, what shall I do to inherit eternal life?" (v. 25).

"What has been written in the Law?" Jesus counterqueried. "How do you read it?"

The lawyer quoted from Leviticus 19:18 and Deuteronomy 6:5, all-out love for God and love of neighbor as for oneself. This initial question which was designed to trap Jesus actually provided Jesus with an opening which the lawyer had not anticipated.

Perhaps to the man's surprise, and certainly to his delight, Jesus responded: "You have answered well," then added: "This do and you shall live."

Then, perhaps now on the defensive, the lawyer inquired: "And who *is* my neighbor?"

Is it necessary to call attention to the strategy which Jesus employed in his response? First of all he mentioned a priest, a member of the Sadducean party, for which the lawyer's party entertained little, if indeed any, respect.

Imagine the Pharisee's reaction when informed that the priest looked the other way and passed by on the other side of the road.

The second traveler was a Levite, also a Sadducee; he might have been one of the staff members of the Temple, or perhaps a caretaker. His indifference in bypassing the unfortunate victim would also bring satisfaction to the pharisaic lawyer.

In that next fleeting second well might the lawyer have experienced a flash of anticipatory satisfaction; who else could the next traveler be but a Pharisee? *He* would surely be that good neighbor. It had to be that way!

But, no! It was someone else. Surely that hated Samaritan would not have stopped to help that fellow; that couldn't be!

Imagine the lawyer's chagrin on learning that the one who did stop was none other than *this despised Samaritan!*

And now, had you noticed the subtle twist which the Lord Jesus has given to the Pharisee's question? "Who is *my* neighbor?" he had inquired. Jesus, however, inquired of him: "Who of these three seems to have been neighbor to the one falling among the thieves?" (v. 36).

Although unwilling to identify the real neighbor as a Samaritan, inasmuch as this despised foreigner had fulfilled the second great commandment which he himself had just quoted for the Master, he acknowledged, though reluctantly: "The one having mercy on him" (v. 37).

Notice also this ironic fact: This man whom the Lord Jesus used as an example of true neighborliness—whether a real or a fictitious character—is known today, not as a good neighbor, but by that designation so offensive to his contemporary Israelitish neighbors as *the good Samaritan!*

And, although he cannot be identified by his real or any other name or title, this good Samaritan still has a challenging message to convey to our advanced civilization—a message of unselfish, unprejudiced, neighborly compassion which is much more challenging than the question with which that Pharisee sought to ensnare Jesus.

Is there any need to repeat this challenging admonition of the Master to that learned lawyer: "You go and do likewise"?

Captive Evangel

2 Kings 5   A mighty man of valour, but . . . a leper.

When this great man came to the king of Israel with a letter from the king of Syria requesting him to cure him of his leprosy, he almost precipitated an international crisis. "He is trying to start a quarrel with me," the king said (v. 8).

Frustrated, Naaman started home. However, he was momentarily detained by the man to whom he had been referred in the first place.

But even after turning to the prophet Elisha, he started home again. Why should he go and dip in that polluted Jordan River? There was plenty of clean water back in Syria. He had expected that prophet to come out and make a big spectacle of the healing of a celebrity of his rank. But that prophet didn't even bother to come out to see him—merely sent word to him.

He would have gone home more disgruntled than ever but for one of his own men whose reasoning turned the failure of this strange mission into success. He boldly reminded Naaman that his lust for spectacular greatness was about to deprive him of something that would enhance his future welfare and usefulness (v. 13).

And still we have not considered the individual who deserves the credit for Naaman's healing. Since the English versions refer to her as "a little maid" (v. 2), she is thought of as a child, a little girl. However, she might have been a young woman, at least an older girl, old enough to be the servant of Naaman's wife.

It was she who suggested that if only her mistress' husband could visit a certain prophet in Israel he could be healed.

Someone overhearing this servant's remark—or could it have been the girl's mistress herself?—passed the word along, and it finally reached the ears of the king himself. He went into action—but without bothering to check with the one who had started the whole thing, with the result that it almost ended in disaster.

Surely this young slave merits a berth among those deserving credit for an example from which posterity can greatly profit.

With reference to the suggestion which she made to her mistress, three things are deserving of note. First of all is her concern for the one who had taken her captive. Her misfortune, bad luck, catastrophy—whatever one might choose to term it—hadn't embittered her, caused her to bemoan her fate, or cause her to "lose her religion."

It would have been easy for her to have developed a sullen, surly attitude toward Naaman and his wife, particularly Naaman, for removing her from her beloved land to this heathen country. She might have had a vengeful, "serves-him-right" attitude, considering it as punishment sent upon him by God for treating her and her people in this manner.

Then there is her reference, in that heathen country where they bowed down to idols, to the Name of Jehovah, the true God. One can appreciate the significance of this by reading what Naaman said to Elisha when he returned to him after being healed: "I know that there is no God in all the earth, but in Israel" (v. 15).

Too much stress cannot be placed upon this girl's remarkable faith in the ministry of God's servant, a faith not shared by the many lepers back in her native land, as the Lord Jesus reminded the people of Nazareth centuries later: "And there were many lepers in Israel at the time of Elisha the prophet, and none of them was cleansed, only Naaman the Syrian" (Luke 4:27).

17

"He would cure him . . . " the maid assured her mistress. "And his flesh was restored like the flesh of a little child" (v. 14).

This girl has bequeathed to posterity something else that we can ill afford to overlook. Many important events have been implemented by the well-timed dropping of observations capitalized upon by others. Credit is not always given where credit is due.

Elisha would not accept the reward offered him by Naaman. What reward or recognition was bestowed upon Naaman's wife's servant for her part in his healing? If any, no record of it has survived. Her most gratifying reward doubtless came in her own mind and heart as she observed the reactions of her mistress—reward surpassing material rewards that might have been bestowed upon her.

Material rewards frequently tarnish or disappear altogether; whereas those deep feelings of satisfaction at having helped others are more meaningful, more durable. To this obscure slave girl we certainly owe a debt of commendation and gratitude.

Benevolent Outcasts

2 Kings 6:24 to 7:20

Not far from where Naaman, commander of the Syrian army, was healed of his leprosy, King Ben-hadad of Syria drew up his military forces against the city of Samaria in one of the worst sieges in the history of Israel. Whether Naaman himself was in command of this expedition we are not informed.

On the verge of starvation, the Samaritans were compelled to eat whatever they could find, even their beasts of burden. One woman, we read, even boiled her own son for food (6:26 ff.).

Outside the city gate were four lepers—among those, incidentally, to whom the Lord Jesus referred when addressing the people of Nazareth (Luke 4:27). Because of their disease, they were forbidden to enter the city or even to mingle with other people.

Realizing that nothing short of starvation awaited them, either outside or inside those city walls, the four decided to throw themselves upon the mercy of those hostile Syrian soldiers.

What had they to lose? "If they save us alive," they reasoned, "then we shall live. And if they kill us, we shall simply die" (2 Kings 7:4).

When they reached the camp of the enemy, however, to their utter amazement, they found it deserted. The Syrians, having heard a strange noise, thinking that reenforcements were coming to the aid of the Samaritans, panicked and fled, leaving behind their tents, food, beasts of burden, and all of their supplies.

Entering one of the tents, the lepers ate and then carried away and hid whatever they wanted from the tent.

Those who, due to circumstances beyond their control, are shunned, looked down upon, ostracized from society, thus hindered from living normal lives, frequently become embittered, not merely against those who treat them in that manner, but against society in general. Well might these four lepers have remained there to enjoy this bonanza, considering this as their opportunity to "get even" by permitting their unfortunate fellow citizens back in the city to starve while they enjoyed life for a change, without having to beg or suffer hunger and privation.

After hiding the spoils from that first tent and returning to a second, they paused to do some serious thinking.

"We're not doing the right thing. This is a day of good news. If we wait till morning, something may happen to us. Let's go and break the news to the king's household" (vv. 7 ff.).

When they arrived at the city gate and broke the news, however, the king discounted the report; this was merely a trick of the enemy to lure them out of the city and overpower them. After all, would it not be human nature for those outcasts to connive with the enemy in order to "get even"?

Then one of the king's servants ventured the suggestion that he dispatch several of his men to investigate. After all, under such trying circumstances as these, what was there to lose? If the men whom he dispatched would be unwilling to risk going over there, they all might starve to death anyway.

The lepers' report, of course, was verified.

And yet all that we know about these four who so generously and unselfishly shared their discovery with their suffering fellow countrymen is that they were outcast lepers. Nor, incidentally, do we know the identity of that servant of the king whose bold, prudent

19

counsel prevented his thwarting God's benevolent provision by discounting the report of these four benevolent outcasts.

Nevertheless, though the four have long since been dead, their benevolence still lives, not only in Old Testament history but also in the minds and hearts of those of us who read the account to remind us not to overlook or disregard those opportunities that may come our way to consider others who are in need of assistance which we may be in a position to provide.

These lepers are also able to drive home the great truth that it is infinitely worthwhile to render needed assistance to those whom we may consider ourselves amply justified in counting undeserving of any gesture of benevolence on our part, merely because of the manner in which they have treated or mistreated us.

This alone makes their unselfish attitude and conduct all the more deserving, not only of note, but of commendation and imitation.

Solicitous Host

Judges 19—21   Do not act so wickedly.

"Every man did that which was right in his own eyes" (21:25).

The significance of these words is vividly portrayed in the closing chapters of the book of Judges. Conduct which was entirely out of harmony with the high standards and commands of God was more in keeping with the standards and practices of those nations which the Israelites had recently replaced. The result was the annihilation of the male members of the tribe of Benjamin.

This account has a familiarly contemporary ring. A Levite had trouble with his concubine. She left him to return to her father's home. After a month, he went to bring her back to his home.

On their way home they stopped overnight in the city of Gibeah, and when no one extended them hospitality they made preparations to spend the night in the street.

An elderly man, not a native of Gibeah, returning from work in the field, found the strangers and extended them an invitation to be his houseguests. When informed that they had food for themselves and provender for their beasts of burden, still the elderly gentleman insisted:

"Just don't stay out in the street," revealing apprehension that harm might come to them.

While they were enjoying this hospitality in his home, a mob, "sons of Belial," "base fellows," came and beat on the door, demanding that the elderly man bring out his guest, "that we may know him" (19:22).

Going out, the host tried to dissuade the mob. He even offered to let them take his own daughter but to no avail.

Then the Levite, whether to show his appreciation to his host or to insure his own safety, permitted them to take his concubine—revealing further evidence of the state of affairs existing in Israel during those dark ages under the Judges.

The following morning, when he opened the door, preparing to leave, he found lying there his concubine's lifeless mutilated body.

He then resorted to a strange course of action. Cutting her body into twelve pieces, he sent a piece to each of the tribes of Israel, to show them what had transpired there in Gibeah.

This strange method of publicity caused a surge of indignation that culminated in almost the complete annihilation of the entire male population of the tribe of Benjamin—and other individuals as well.

As a result of this mass action, the men of Israel came together for a mass prayer meeting before the Lord, deploring the state of affairs existing in their land.

With such deplorable conditions existing in Israel, how could one fail to be impressed with the hospitality of this fine elderly resident of Gibeah whose attitude was so vastly different from that of his contemporaries, causing him to stand out like a beautiful lily springing up in a stagnant pond or a refreshing breeze in sweltering heat— willing to sacrifice his own daughter to prevent those "sons of Belial" from infringing upon his hospitality—even though his guest prevented him from doing so?

One wonders what such a man as he might have been and done if he had lived in a more wholesome and godly environment.

Assuredly this man of old has a timely, worthwhile message to convey over the centuries to those of our day, which in many respects seems not to be too far removed from the type of environment in which he was living.

Devoted and Devout

Genesis 24

The outstanding characteristic of the Patriarch Abraham, counted to him, as the apostle Paul points out as righteousness (Gal. 3:6), was faith in God, demonstrated, for example, by his willingness to offer his only son, Isaac, as a sacrifice to God.

Coupled with his faith was his faithfulness to God. And this is demonstrated by his concern for the future of that son. Determined that Isaac must not marry one of the young women of Canaan, he commissioned his oldest most trusted servant to go and secure a bride for Isaac, a commission from which he would not be released unless the young woman should refuse to come with him and marry Isaac.

To seek that bride, this servant was to return to Abraham's homeland. However, he was not to take Isaac with him. Although in keeping with Oriental custom, still practiced in some countries, this instruction can also be interpreted as Abraham's awareness of the weakness of Isaac, who obviously lacked much of his father's strength of character. It is also indicative of Abraham's confidence in his veteran servant's loyalty and trustworthiness.

We have as a result one of the most unusual and fascinating proxy-love stories in the entire Bible—or for that matter anywhere else, even more fascinating than the story of Miles Standish. This is the more intriguing because of this veteran servant's dual loyalty, making him the type of person whom one would greatly appreciate having in one's employ—even knowing by name.

He made careful preparations for this special assignment by first collecting the necessary supplies for the journey and then selecting gifts for the prospective bride and her family.

Arriving at the city of Nahor in Mesopotamia, he realized the need of something more. And so he turned to his master's God and prayed a specific prayer, even to the very details (vv. 12-14).

Hardly had he concluded that prayer when along came the answer in the person of a young lady named Rebekah, of whom he requested a drink of water and then stood there waiting in anticipation and anxiety.

This servant's character is further revealed in his reaction to this miraculous answer to his prayer. Now he wants to know her identity and whether there is room for both his party and himself to spend the night at her house!

Still there is more. While this answer to his prayer is watering his camels, he takes time out to voice his deep, sincere gratitude to God for so wonderful a manifestation of divine graciousness. At a wonderful moment like this, how many of us would pause to express gratitude to God? One out of ten, perhaps?

The man's character stands out even more clearly when contrasted with that of Rebekah's brother, Laban. Laban became so fascinated by the jewelry which the servant had already given Rebekah that he hurried out to extend cordial hospitality to the servant, who had bowed his head and worshiped God once more, for this marvelous answer to his prayer.

Nor is he satisfied to enjoy this hospitality any longer than is absolutely necessary. Although they insist upon his tarrying for ten days to give Rebekah time to prepare for her departure, he insists upon leaving the following morning; he considers it necessary that he return immediately to inform his master of the wonderful success of his mission.

The servant's identity? He too must be classified among those who, having served commendably, have slipped into anonymity— but by no means into total obscurity. His remarkable example, worthy of emulation for several reasons, is deserving of widespread publicity in the hope that it may be emulated in an era in which everyone is diligently striving to "do his own thing" rather than endeavoring to assist others in doing theirs.

This man has not only left to us an outstanding example of his own but, because of his conduct, has paid a glowing tribute also to his master, whose devotion to God was such as to inspire in this servant that same devotion and dependence.

Widow of Sarepta

1 Kings 17:8 ff.

On his first visit to his home town of Nazareth after beginning his public ministry, why did Jesus call special attention to this widow of Sarepta (or Zarephath)? (Luke 4:26).

The Lord had several plausible reasons which make this an interesting study in contrast.

Have you ever stepped upon foreign soil? If so, what was your initial reaction? That strange sensation of being a foreigner, an alien? Or have you ever entertained or had dealings with an alien?

If so, surely you are in a better position to appreciate this widow's reactions when approached by a foreigner, particularly an Israelite, for they were not always friendly toward people of other nations.

This alien approached the widow in a very unusual manner. He requested her to go home and bake him a cake when there was hardly enough meal for her and her son, with the prospect of nothing more in sight except starvation. Furthermore, he assured her that as long as he remained with them there would be no lack of food.

It certainly required a great deal of courage and faith for her to comply with that foreigner's strange request. Nevertheless she did so, and during Elijah's entire sojourn in that home, there was no lack of food; all three of them fared well.

On his initial visit to Nazareth during his ministry, Jesus was greeted with a demonstration of skepticism. No one from *their* city could do all of the things which they were hearing about *him*. Why was he not doing some of those strange things here at home?

The residents of Nazareth should have been familiar with this incident to which Jesus referred. After warning King Ahab that there would be no rain in Israel for a period of three and a half years, Elijah went down to the Brook Kidron where he remained and was fed by ravens till the brook dried up, at which time God directed him to go over to Sarepta.

There things went well—till the widow's son died. Then she began to question Elijah. Why had things turned out this way? Why did this happen to her?

Taking the boy's body up to his room, Elijah laid it on the bed and began to pray. God answered that prayer.

And when that mother saw her son alive again, she said to Elijah: "Now I know that you are a man of God" (v. 24).

This event took place, it should not be forgotten, back in those days when God was still dealing solely with the Israelites. Those nations round about were considered outside the fold, and those nations thought that Israel's God, Jehovah, was limited in power to that one nation, but powerless beyond its borders, as Ben-hadad and his fighting men learned to their sorrow (see 1 Kings 20:23 ff.).

Here, therefore, we meet one of those specially-favored foreigners about whom we read throughout the Old Testament, on whom God showered his grace and mercy, revealing once more that he is interested in and concerned about *all* of us human beings.

And there in Nazareth people had been specially favored and privileged to observe the Son of God growing up into manhood in their very midst, aware that he had gone out of their midst and performed all of those wonderful miracles which were impossible for ordinary human beings to perform. Nevertheless they were now scoffing, ridiculing, criticizing, ousting, and actually trying to destroy him by pushing him over the crest of the hill.

And so as a reminder, an example, and as a rebuke to the people of his hometown, Jesus holds up in vivid contrast the experience of this foreign widow and her son.

Should we not add that this is a challenge also to many of our own day who, in the light of all that God, through his Son and his Holy Spirit, has done for mankind through these many centuries, still reject the promised Messiah?

Host Unaware

Luke 2:1-7 . . . no room in the inn.

Heard particularly during the Christmas season, these familiar words furnish the only explanation for the birth of Jesus in a manger and of his having a feeding trough as a cradle.

Why was the Son of God born in such unusual surroundings? Ostensibly it was due to the fact that the Roman emperor had issued a decree that a census be taken and that everyone must return to his or her birthplace.

Therefore when Joseph and Mary arrived in Bethlehem, they were greeted with words familiar to us today, "NO VACANCY."

This Bethlehem inn, though by no means so elaborate, might be considered as a forerunner of our modern motels; camels and donkeys were parked outside in stalls, while travelers went into the courtyard for their places of lodging.

Whether or not this innkeeper was the one who offered the manger to this couple or whether all of his stalls were also occupied and Joseph and Mary had to search elsewhere, we are not informed.

When the anxious bridegroom turned away to search for a place in which this highly-favored virgin might be delivered of her firstborn, what transpired? Since they now resided in Nazareth, perhaps they were not too well acquainted in Bethlehem, now whither should he turn for aid or advice? Perhaps he had already been searching for lodging.

And what about the attitude of this innkeeper? Had he been brusque and hard-boiled due to the increased activity during this rush? Or had he treated Joseph kindly because of Mary's condition? Had Joseph informed him, perhaps reminding him of the Old Testament prophecy which, as he and Mary knew, would be fulfilled here in Bethlehem at this time? Had he done so, would this innkeeper have believed his report? (Isa. 53:1 ff.).

After learning who they really were, what was this inkeeper's reaction? As the author of Hebrews reminds us, people have entertained angels without being conscious of the fact (Heb. 13:2).

"If I had only known!" When coming from great depths, this time-worn exclamation carries much more profound meaning than can be realized by those who hear the words. In later years, when reports came in concerning this Christ child who might have been in the innkeeper's establishment instead of out there in that manger, how did this man react?

Even in this small community, how swiftly did the news spread without the aid of newspapers, telephones, radios, and televisions? Was this reported merely as another birth?

All that we learn from Luke is contained in one phrase in one verse (2:18), "And all those hearing marvelled . . ." (v. 18). But whether the innkeeper was among them we are not informed.

Those shepherds from out on the hills arrived that same night after learning of the Messiah's birth, but with how much fanfare we are not informed.

Can't you almost hear this inkeeper exclaiming: "Why, if I had known who they actually were I think I would have turned out someone already inside my inn and let them find other quarters! Yes, and I'd even have given them my own quarters and gone out there and spent the night."

Absurd? On the contrary, quite plausible!

And yet this man need not have censured himself too severely for turning them away. Was this not, after all, in keeping with Jesus' purpose in coming into this world, not to be served, but to serve? Had God so desired, could he not have selected Herod's palace or the Temple, as those Wise Men from the East who came looking for Jesus were positive that so important an event would certainly take place?

How much or how little this man's life was changed by this historic event we can only conjecture. However, it can affect us; we too are given opportunities to entertain messengers of God unaware. Yet, like this man, we may blindly pass them up, only to realize too late our failure to take advantage of opportunities that might have wrought significant changes in our subsequent living.

The best way to be in a position to take advantage of such opportunities is to sustain such a relationship with God that the Holy Spirit will be able to supply the needed direction on the strength of that sterling quality on our part which is mentioned in Hebrews 11:1—*faith*.

Worldly Wise

Matthew 2:1-12   Wise men from the East arrived in Jerusalem (v. 1).

Based upon the types of gifts which they presented when they worshiped the newborn King, tradition has it that there were three of them. Matthew, however, does not record their number. All that is definitely known is that there were two or more.

He describes them as being magi.[1] This is the word used of a man named Simon who attracted the attention of people in Samaria by practicing magic and sorcery (Acts 8:9 ff.), also of a Jewish magician or sorcerer who tried to attract people by means of deception (Acts 13:6 ff.).

But these men from the East were astrologers, as we infer from their declaration: ". . . For we saw his star in the East and have come to worship him" (v. 2). There were known to be astrologers in Persia and the East at that time.

Their claim that they had seen *"his* star" need not raise any doubt or question as to their integrity or sincerity. This was one of those divinely given signs heralding the descent of his Son into the world, as was the appearance of that angelic chorus to those shepherds out on the Judean hills on that eventful night.

Due to the means of travel in those times, these men undoubtedly arrived in Jerusalem sometime after the birth of Jesus. Whether that star had appeared to them before, at the time of, or after the birth of Jesus we are not informed. That he was born before their arrival in Jerusalem is indicated by their question (v. 2).

Evidently they went directly to King Herod's palace. Where else would this new King of the Jews be likely to be born?

And when Herod heard about the birth of a new King of Israel, he became greatly perturbed and immediately began making investigation of his own. Calling together the scribes and chief priests, he asked where their newborn King was supposed to be born.

The Pharisees and Sadducees had very little to do with each other, and neither party, particularly the Sadducees, had respect for the Roman authorities who occupied their land at that time. Even if they had learned of Jesus' birth, because of Herod's reputation as a ruthless man who would not hesitate to do away with anyone who he thought might jeopardize his position, they doubtless would not have disclosed the information to him. They merely informed him that the Christ child was to be born in Bethlehem.

If these Wise Men had gone immediately to the Temple, they could have learned firsthand where this event was to take place. As a matter of fact, they might even have found the royal family there, for after the days of purification, they brought their newborn child to the Temple and presented him to his Father (see Luke 2:22-38).

At the time when these Wise Men finally arrived in Bethlehem, they found the newborn King, not out there in that manger, but in a house; people who had come back to be enrolled because of the census had gone home, and there was now room for the family (v. 11).

These wise stargazers not only caused that commotion in Jerusalem but they also precipitated a disastrous situation in Bethlehem. When Herod learned from those Jewish authorities that their promised King was to be born in Bethlehem, he secretly instructed these Wise Men to return to Jerusalem after finding the Christ child and report to him— "that I too may go and worship him" (v. 8).

When, after a considerable lapse of time, they did not return (v. 12), certain that they had disregarded his request, Herod sent soldiers to Bethlehem with instructions to massacre every male child under two years of age, so as to be certain that they wouldn't overlook the newborn King. This is further indication that doubtless considerable time had elapsed between the birth of Jesus and the appearance of these astrologers.

Could these Wise Men have been proselytes of Judaism? There were many of them in those days. This raises a further question which seems to be overlooked by many. Inasmuch as they recognized "his star" in the east, why were they not familiar with the place where he was to be born? Was it because they relied upon their own wisdom, reasoning that there could be only one place where so important a celebrity as the King of the Jews was likely to be born—the city of Jerusalem?

This delay and difficulty undoubtedly could have been averted, and things could have been different if somewhere along the way they had not taken their eyes off that guiding star and relied on their own wisdom; for on the way from Jerusalem they once more saw that star "and rejoiced exceedingly" (v. 10).

These Wise Men can therefore convey to people of our day a vitally important message, which is summed up in these familiar words written by that man of Wisdom: "Trust in the Lord, and do not rely upon your own understanding" (Prov. 3:5).

What confusion, delay, and extra travel for themselves, and what trouble, difficulty, and misery they could have spared others had they kept their gaze fixed on that star and relied, not on their own wisdom, but on the wisdom and power of him who had placed that star out there for their special guidance. For so far as we are informed, they were the only ones who saw the star, which finally rested above the place where the Christ child was lying.

Is it not wonderful that when we humans fail to put our trust in God, he, in his grace, wisdom, and lovingkindness, is able and willing to provide a remedy, a way out? God warned the magi to avoid reporting to Herod and to return home by another route.

Furthermore, God also instructed Joseph to take the newly born child down into Egypt and to remain there until after the death of Herod the Great (vv. 19-26).

No human power or authority was able or permitted to destroy him who, before returning to his heavenly Father, declared: "All authority (power) was given to me in heaven and upon the earth . . ." (Matt. 28:19).

[1] Greek word *magoi.*

Sightseers

Luke 2:8-20   Now let's go over and see this thing (v. 15).

How many people have ever seen an angel coming down from heaven and speaking directly to them? How many people have listened to a chorus of angels singing for their special benefit?

What a glorious privilege accorded these shepherds out there on those Judean hills that night! What a glorious spectacle! What a thrilling revelation!

"Let's go over to Bethlehem and see this thing for ourselves!" they decided after talking it over.

Having made this decision, they left their flocks and went into Bethlehem. How thrilling it was to walk in and announce to those who were present that they had been given this amazing opportunity of hearing the good news from heaven that Immanuel had come down to this earth to live in the flesh. How the shepherds were privileged to join this little select group to welcome the Christ child!

The happy mother, we read, "stored up all these things in her heart," where she would be storing many more wonderful things in the future.

All that we learn further from Luke, the only Gospel writer who has recorded this incident, is that these shepherds returned to their flocks, glorifying and praising God. What permanent effect this phenomenal experience had upon them must remain a matter of mere speculation.

Did this experience merely become one of those exciting stories to be rehashed out there in the lonely stillness of those dark nights, such as this one started to be, until in the course of time it would lose much of its original glamor, perhaps become almost unrecognizable? Surely it would not be permitted to vanish into forgetfulness—or would it?

Oh, well, why bother about it after all these centuries, in the light of the many other things that crowd in to claim our attention? Was this perhaps the attitude of those highly favored shepherds as they settled down to the lonely routine of watching over their sheep?

So far as can be learned from the Scriptures, after that eventful episode, they dropped into obscurity. Whether in later years they became followers of the Christ child we do not know. Nor do we, of course, know their names—they are merely referred to as shepherds; we do not even know how many of them there were.

The Lord Jesus has left us that well-known parable of a shepherd who, having ninety-nine of his sheep back in the fold, nevertheless went out to look for one lost sheep. He also referred to himself as the Good Shepherd. Has it ever occurred to you that among the twelve disciples there was not one shepherd?

In their failure to follow through and take advantage of this unique opportunity, did not these favored shepherds actually "miss the boat?" Is this not the message which these unidentified shepherds can convey to our contemporaries, not merely that which they themselves witnessed back there that night but also what they failed to derive from that initial, and quite evidently final, experience?

What a testimony they could have given through those years between that glorious night and the time of Jesus' wonderful ministry! And what a wonderful ministry they themselves could have had after Jesus' resurrection and the coming of the Holy Spirit! But were they present to witness those glorious events? Who knows?

Just as those two sets of brothers were called to become fishers of men, as they are still known today, so these unidentified men might have become shepherds of human sheep.

They can, of course, remind us of the many opportunities which we too have to tell what we ourselves have experienced—not having of course seen the Christ child lying there in that manger, but of receiving the good news and relating our own experience of having him come into and transforming our own lives and giving us eternal life from above. Is this not even more wonderful than seeing and hearing those angels in the sky?

How much it means for us to yield ourselves to the Holy Spirit so as to have a greater part in carrying this wonderful message to multitudes who are still wandering about as sheep without a shepherd. Let's capitalize on our opportunities and, in the language of Simon Peter to that lame beggar outside the Temple, give them what we have (see Acts 3:6).

Inquiring Reporters

Matthew 11:4-6; Luke 7:18-23   Are you the coming one, or do we wait for another?

This is the message which was sent to Jesus by the one who just a short time previous had boldly proclaimed the coming of the Son of God who would baptize, not with water, but with fire and with the Holy Spirit. And when the One greater than he came upon the scene, John pointed him out, baptized him and, in keeping with the promise of God, saw the Spirit of God descending upon him in the form of a dove (Matt. 3:16).

Could the one who was doing all those wonderful things really be the Promised One to whom John had been so faithful in foretelling to multitudes of Israelites that he would be coming?

Or had he been mistaken? If he *were* the promised Messiah, why would he permit him to languish here in prison? Doubtless many such thoughts passed through the mind of John the Baptist in that lonely prison prompting him to send these two men out to see and investigate, and bring back a firsthand report.

When these messengers came to Jesus, he was healing and proclaiming the good news of salvation. And when they told him what they had been sent to inquire, Jesus went on doing those things. Was he deliberately ignoring them, brushing them off? On the contrary, he was giving them a demonstration, furnishing them with material for the report which they were to carry back to the disheartened forerunner, which he should be able to recognize as what he himself had foretold to those multitudes who had come to listen to his message.

Then the promised Messiah turned and instructed these messengers to return to their teacher with a firsthand report, not only of what they had heard from him, but what they had actually observed him doing.

Of what importance or value is the mission of these disciples of John the Baptist to us today? The answer is that similar questions which John the Baptist posed are frequently being asked also by many people today. "Why did God permit this to happen to me?" "Why does God let me suffer this way?" "Why should I deserve such treatment as this?"

After John had faithfully carried out his mission, why did the promised Messiah permit him finally to be beheaded at the request of a dancer whose mother was enraged by his bold rebuke of her present husband for having taken her from his brother? (see Matt. 14:1-12; Mark 6:14-29; Luke 9:7-9).

The most logical and honest answer to such questions, even though not the most acceptable, is that we mortals do not actually *know* the answers to such questions. Nevertheless, of one thing we *can* and *should* be certain. Although here on earth we do have trials, tribulations, and suffering, this is not the end. Jesus has promised more wonderful things in that place which he has gone to prepare for us and which he came down to earth to make available, *through such intense suffering and humiliation,* to us.

On one occasion he said to his disciples that if he, the Son of God, was treated as he was, how much *more* could they expect from sinful, rebellious human beings?

We learn something else growing out of the coming of these two

33

disciples of John, something which we also learn, of course, from the life of the Lord Jesus himself. The manner in which we endure our own trials, sufferings, and afflictions frequently means much more to others than we may realize. Was this included in what the Master meant when he said: "He who endures to the end shall be saved?" (Matt. 10:22; 24:13).

The message which Jesus sent with these disciples of John is just as important for the people of our day. It is just as important to those skeptics who refuse to acknowledge that Jesus *is* the Son of God, the Messiah who came into this world to reveal God's will and manifest God's love. Taking our place on Calvary's cross—not because of *his own* sin, but of humanity's—Jesus still proclaims to bring lost humanity into the fold of God, rising from the dead, thus conquering death for those who will put their trust in and manifest their faith in him.

Separated from Jesus by those prison walls, the only way in which John the Baptist was able to learn the answer to his doubts concerning Jesus was through these messengers.

We who are separated from what these messengers saw and heard, not by prison walls, but by intervening centuries of time, must in like manner accept their report, *all* of their reports concerning Jesus' earthly ministry, just as did John, by *faith.*

They who exercise this faith and acknowledge Jesus Christ as the promised Messiah who fulfilled all of those prophecies concerning him, just as did many in those days who saw, heard, and trusted in him as their Savior and Lord, receive eternal life in and through him by the power of the Holy Spirit.

Who were these two disciples of John? We are not informed. Nor were they informed that the report which they carried back to John there in that prison would also be transmitted to posterity through the centuries to follow.

Interrupted Funeral

Luke 7:11-17   And the corpse sat up and began to speak.

As far removed from this scene as we are, would it be possible to visualize and fully appreciate so strange a phenomenon?

Wouldn't it be interesting to learn what this youth said when suddenly he sat up and began talking? "Where am I?" "What happened?" "What am I doing here?" "What's going on here anyway?" "What are all these people doing out here?"

And wouldn't you like to know how his mother reacted when the Lord Jesus delivered her son to her, *alive once more?* Luke has not recorded any of the details for us, although he has described the reactions of the large crowd that had made up that funeral procession. The multitude that had been following Jesus were seized with fear—obvious reaction to such an unprecedented phenomenon, a dead youth suddenly sitting up and beginning to speak! Who besides God could possibly perform so marvelous a miracle? "Surely there must be a prophet in our midst!"

As would be expected, news of this unprecedented event spread as rapidly as the limited facilities of communication of that era permitted. Luke informs us that the report spread all over Judea and out to the surrounding regions— "A dead boy on the way to his grave suddenly sat up and began speaking!"

In the wake of so miraculous an experience, what became of this lad and his mother? Did they return to their home there in Nain, taking up where they had left off at his death, to enjoy life with renewed interest, new zest? Did this strange experience soon lose its significance as they mingled with their relatives, friends, and neighbors who had made up that funeral procession and witnessed that wonderful miracle?

Suppose mother and son had joined that multitude that was following Jesus, joyfully sharing their testimony with those who had not witnessed the event? She said, "We were on our way to the grave, when the Teacher came up and stopped the procession and brought back my son from the dead!" "Just think!" he exclaimed, "all of a sudden I found myself sitting up in that coffin and talking! Isn't it wonderful?"

How effective their personal testimony would have been of the wonderful power of the Son of God—not merely over life, but also over death itself!

Nothing further, however, is reported concerning this mother and her restored son, unless it is couched in such general statements as "a great multitude followed him," or "many put their trust in him."

We read further about Lazarus and his two sisters after his marvelous return from the grave, about Mary Magdalene, about that healed blind man who could not be silenced even by the threat of excommunication from the synagogue, that healed leper who, even though admonished by Jesus to tell nobody, couldn't keep his mouth closed, went everywhere telling everybody about it.

"If I had lived back there in Jesus' day," someone is occasionally heard to say, "and heard him speak and witnessed his miracles, I might have believed in him." Here were two who had not only seen and heard, but *had actually experienced* the demonstration of his miraculous power. But like those thousands who partook of that boy's meager lunch, went their own way, so far as we know, and permitted the great Miracle worker to go his.

Who was this youth? Who was his widowed mother, whose grief over her son's death had been intense, as indicated by the large crowd of sympathizers attending her son's interrupted funeral?

There is but one answer: "Identity unknown."

And so this boy, now twice dead, can convey to posterity a negative message such as: "Don't make the mistake my mother and I made, selfishly withholding our wonderful testimony which could have benefitted so many others of our day."

How many parents, other loved ones, and friends, overcome by grief, would cherish this experience of seeing their loved ones restored to life! And yet many of them do not even have the assurance that they will ever again see those departed ones because they have not put their trust in the Lord Jesus who, although he does not now bring people back from the realm of the dead, has promised a better life hereafter to those of us who put our trust in him.

Uncontrollable

Mark 1:40-45[1] If you desire, you can cleanse me.

But for that dread disease, what sort of persons would lepers have been? Compelled to live apart from other people, compelled to display a sign indicating that they had that dread disease, crying "unclean,

36

unclean!" when approached by anyone, how had their isolation affected their personalities?

Mark, in this opening chapter of his Gospel has left us the account of one of these lepers who had an experience quite different from many others whom Jesus healed. All that we actually know about him is that he manifested an unusually aggressive attitude.

Kneeling before Jesus, he uttered words revealing mingled confidence, expectation, and determination: "If you desire (if you want to do it), you can cleanse me."

Whether or not he had previously seen or heard of others who had experienced or witnessed the Lord's healing power, or whether he was exercising an aggressive faith which some have and others lack, we have no way of knowing. What we do know, however, is that his faith was rewarded.

Moved with compassion, the Master answered: "I do desire. Be made clean." And stretching out his hand, he *touched* that leper—doubtless the first time anyone had ever touched him. And with that touch the leprosy disappeared.

Then the Master added a strange admonition: "See to it that you say nothing to anybody, but go away, show yourself to the priest and make and offering for your cleansing which Moses arranged for an offering to them" (v. 44).

Mark describes the manner in which Jesus dismissed the man with a word that has several possible sharp, severe, irritable meanings, either because he knew what this healed man was going to do or, as has been suggested, because of the severity of that dread disease—perhaps even a combination of the two.

Nevertheless, this stern admonition notwithstanding, the man was so elated over what the Healer had done for him that he went all out spreading the good news everywhere, with the result that people from all around came bringing their sick and afflicted. And due to the crowds that came, Jesus found it necessary to stay away from the cities, but stayed out in the desert places, and the people even came out there from everywhere (v. 45).

In view of the phenomenal results of this leper's zealous efforts, for what reason did the Lord admonish him not to tell anybody about his healing? And what does Mark mean by declaring that so many were being brought to be healed that Jesus could not even enter the cities?

The answer is undoubtedly found in what Mark has recorded in connection with the incident immediately preceding this. On the morning after the Lord Jesus had healed Simon Peter's mother-in-law, just as on the previous evening (following the sabbath), people were bringing many sick and afflicted to be healed. However, when the disciples awoke, they were unable to locate the Master.

When finally they located him, he was in a lonely place, praying. Wasn't he aware that back there in Capernaum multitudes were looking for him?

His unexpected response was, "Let's go somewhere else, into the neighboring villages, that I may proclaim the Good News there also, because for this purpose have I come forth" (v. 38).

Many people were following him for the loaves and fishes, many others for the healing of their bodies, yet others out of curiosity, to see what wonderful miracles he would perform next. Comparatively few manifested real interest in the most important, most valuable gift which the Messiah had to offer them, redemption of their immortal souls.

Had Jesus merely healed people's bodies, catered to their physical appetites, and satisfied their curiosity, how far short would he have come of fulfilling that primary mission which had brought him down to earth!

But why, then, did the Lord not permit that healed Gerasene demoniac to leave with him but tell him to stay there and go home and tell his people what he had done for him? (see Mark 5:19).

That was a different situation. In Capernaum people were familiar with his healing ministry; this healed leper had nothing new to communicate to them.

Suppose this healed enthusiast had lingered and listened to the Messiah's good news concerning the healing and redemption of the soul. (Had he done so, surely Mark or one of the other Gospel narrators would have recorded it.) The most for which we could hope is that after the resurrection of Jesus and the coming of the Holy Spirit, he was among those thousands whose souls were also healed and cleansed from the leprosy of sin.

Nevertheless, he too can speak across these many centuries, particularly to those who would advocate a "social gospel" to the neglect of the evangelistic ministry of the spiritually redeemed, in keeping with Jesus' Great Commission (Matt. 28:19-20).

We can, to be sure, have both of these ministries. However, we can ill afford to major on the physical and material to the neglect of the more vitally important eternal spiritual, as many in our day are doing.

How greatly the kingdom work of our Lord and Savior Jesus Christ could be advanced if more of his followers were to display this healed leper's faith and zeal. And had he been healed spiritually, he might now be identified by name, instead of merely as a zealous healed leper.

¹ And Matthew 8:2-4; Luke 5:12-16.

One Out of Ten

Luke 17:11-19   And where are the other nine?

Due to their isolation from the rest of society, lepers had fellowship with each other. Enroute to Jerusalem, Jesus was accosted by ten lepers. Stopping at a respectable distance, they called out: "Master Jesus, have mercy on us" (v. 13).

Jesus told them to go and show themselves to the priest (in Jerusalem). And as they went, they discovered that they were miraculously healed.

Jesus' telling them to go and show themselves to the priest implies that as many as nine of them were Israelites and were required by the Mosaic law to present an offering for their ceremonial cleansing.

Expressions of gratitude do not always come from expected sources. It seems so easy to take things for granted, to be so confident that we are deserving of things which we need or desire. When these things are received, we neglect to register the gratitude of which our benefactors are deserving. We enjoy the favors and forget those who have made them available.

On the other hand, when expressions of gratitude come from unexpected sources, we are amazed—as greatly as we are disappointed when they do not come from expected sources.

Why give so much attention to this incident which is so well-known? There are actually several reasons.

Why was it, we may inquire, that this tenth leper was the only one who returned to express his thanks to his Healer?

The only one of these ten lepers whose nationality is actually mentioned is this one man who returned to express his gratitude. He was not a member of the chosen race of Israel, but a member of that hybrid race despised and avoided by the Israelites; he was a Samaritan.

Was he grateful because he, a despised Samaritan, was included in those healed by the Jewish Messiah? Or was it because of his inherent nature?

For either reason, or perhaps both, this alien stands out prominently, because he was thoughtful and courteous enough to return and pour out his thanks to his Healer. Glorifying God in a loud voice, he fell on his face before Jesus' feet and poured out his thanks to him (vv. 15-16).

He stands out not only among these ten, but among many beneficiaries, most of whom went their merry way without bothering to return and express their gratitude.

Among the most outstanding experiences which the Master had were those involving, not Israelites, but foreigners. And on one occasion he declared that those who have received the greatest blessings are the ones most likely to give expression of their appreciation.

It should be pointed out also that giving expression to sincere gratitude has a wholesome effect upon the personalities of those who, like this healed Samaritan, are so thoughtful and considerate. Selfish, greedy thoughtlessness takes its toll from an individual's character and personality.

In like manner, expressions of gratitude, or their absence, have their effect upon the benefactors. People have been known to question whether good deeds which they have done for others were actually worthwhile, due to the apparent carelessness or indifference with which they have been received—not necessarily because they were eager to be thanked or rewarded but because of their uncertainty as to whether or not their efforts were actually welcomed or really necessary. They might even be hesitant about aiding others in the future.

In the light of this episode, there may be ground for the assertion made by someone that ingratitude is at least one of the humanity's unpardonable sins.

And how frequently do we humans think to pause and express our gratitude to God for his many gracious favors, in the manner in which this grateful Samaritan thanked the Son of God?

Victim

Mark 3:1-6[1]   And they watched him . . . .

Had this man come to the synagogue that sabbath day with the intention of worshiping? Or was it with the hope that this Healer about whom everyone was talking would be there and would possibly heal his hand?

Was the man aware that he would be used by those conniving Pharisees and Sadducees who were seeking further evidence against Jesus for disregarding their sabbath tradition?

Those strict legalists were there, watching to learn whether Jesus would heal the man on the sabbath. In fact, Matthew informs us that they actually asked him: "Is it lawful to heal on the sabbath day?" (12:10), that they might trap him.

Jesus in turn inquired of them whether one of them would not rescue a sheep that would fall into a pit on the sabbath, then inquired as to how much more valuable a human being was than a sheep (Matt. 12:12).

Knowing their desire to find reasons for doing away with him, the Lord Jesus then inquired, "I ask you, is it lawful on the sabbath to do good, or to do harm? to save a life, or to destroy it?" (Luke 6:9). Then he proceeded to heal the man which, incidentally, required a minimum of effort on his part.

Of how much more effort, exertion, work were those Pharisees guilty that same day in their efforts to do away with Jesus than he exerted in healing the man with a withered hand?

Regardless of his reason for being in that synagogue that sabbath day, this man was actually being used by those legalists as an exhibit of Jesus' healing on that day, because, despite Jesus' sound reasoning, they left the synagogue and began plotting with the Sadducees— for whom they had no particular respect or affection—to do away with the Messiah.

This incident could have placed this man in an embarrassing and dangerous position. Like that blind man whom Jesus healed (John 9), he could have been expelled from the synagogue unless, like that cripple whom the Lord healed on the sabbath, he had turned against his Healer in order to save his own reputation and perhaps his own life (John 5), for breaking the sabbath by carrying home his bed.

Who was this healed man, and what became of him? Inasmuch as we do not have the answers to such questions, why trouble ourselves about him? What worthwhile message could he possibly convey to posterity?

Just this, the possibility that one in his position can easily be used, whether willingly or even unwittingly, to bring criticism, perhaps even bodily harm to one who is, or could be his benefactor. Yes, and as in this case, it is possible for one to be used by others to bring reproach upon the Lord Jesus himself to whom we owe so great a debt of gratitude.

This man cannot be commended, certainly, for his failure to take a definite stand with his divine Healer. If he had done so, surely we would have been informed of this in one of the Gospels.

His case does bring into focus once more the Lord's reason for turning away from those crowds in Capernaum who sought bodily healing or from those who desired to make him King because of his ability to feed multitudes with a boy's meager lunch. These miracles were designed to prove to them, and to us, that he was God's Son—that his primary reason for coming to earth was to bring eternal life.

Thus his message could well be something like this: "Be careful not to permit yourselves to be used by those who would injure or harm others, particularly your benefactors, and especially your Supreme Benefactor."

[1] And Matthew 12:9-14; Luke 6:6-11.

Ingrate

John 5:1-16   The one healing me told me . . . .

That this man who had been ill for thirty-eight years wanted to be healed is clearly evident from his being there at the Pool of Bethzatha [1] and by his response to the Lord Jesus' question that he had no one to push him into the pool. Tradition was that the first one entering the pool whenever the water bubbled up would be healed. His serious condition is emphasized by his inability to move down into the water before someone else reached it.

How frequently he had been brought there to the pool John has not informed us.

The healing of the man was simple. Without touching him, the Master said, "Get up, pick up your bed (mat) and walk about." And without hesitation the man did so.

Immediately he found himself in trouble. Pharisees saw him carrying his bed, in violation of their sabbath tradition, and demanded to know why he was doing so, to which he answered:

"The man who healed me told me to do it."

However, when they asked who the one was who had healed him, he was unable to tell them, for Jesus had immediately slipped away into the crowd at the pool. [2]

Those legalists were concerned more about the man's violation of their sabbath tradition than elated over the healing of the man who had suffered for nearly two-score years. Whatever reaction the healed man himself was experiencing, which, incidentally, John has not recorded, was overshadowed by the prospect of the possible punishment that might be meted out to him. According to their legalistic system, this could have been as severe as stoning to death if they had so desired.

If he had left his bed there at the pool till after sundown, it might not have been there when he returned to pick it up.

The man's character is revealed by his readiness to shift his sabbath violation upon Jesus Christ, the one who had made it possible for him, not only to be able to pick up and carry that bed, but to be

43

able to get up and walk away under his own power.

Later Jesus met the man in the Temple. "Look," he told him, you have been healed; don't go on sinning any more, lest something worse come to you" (v. 14).

Although Jesus did not spell out what that worse calamity might be, we can make several deductions. It has been suggested, for example, that his physical condition might have been caused by his having sinned; many people suffer physically as well as otherwise because of their violation of God's laws and commandments.

Then again, Jesus was giving the man the same opportunity which he gave that blind man whom he also healed and encountered later in the Temple (John 9). Certainly rejection of the opportunity of receiving eternal life is the greatest of all sins, and this man, instead of heeding the counsel of the Healer of his body, left the Temple and, in order to escape possible punishment for carrying his mat on the sabbath, went and informed those Pharisees that he now knew who had told him to do that.

It meant more to the man to be a living coward than a martyr—if indeed those legalists would have gone to the trouble of having him punished; their concern was seeking to do away with his Healer, and now he was another living example to whom they would be able to point.

This calls to mind the Master's admonition on another occassion: "And do not be afraid of those killing the body but not being able to kill the soul; but fear rather the One able to destroy both soul and body in gehenna" [3] (Matt. 10:28).

What genuine satisfaction could this healed cripple have had during the remainder of his life, living with the knowledge that he had actually betrayed his Benefactor, the Son of the living God? Although he was enjoying new health, there was that realization that, because of his desire to save his own reputation, he had been the cause of increased persecution of his benefactor by those Pharisees, who seemingly did not care that he was now able to walk.

This is the message which he can still convey—a negative message. It is possible to have within one's grasp the prospect of everlasting life and yet to reject it in the eagerness to hold on to and enjoy the prospect of a prolonged, yet temporary earthly life.

44

What a great opportunity the man rejected—enjoying the best that Jesus had to offer him—*life eternal.*

[1] Some manuscripts have "Bethesda," others "Bethsaida."
[2] The Greek word used here *(kolumbethra)* suggests that this could have been a swimming pool.
[3] Gehenna—the place of everlasting punishment.

Gratitude—and Grit

John 9

Try to visualize this man's reactions as, surrounded by Jesus' disciples and perhaps others, he listens to such questions as "who sinned to bring on this condition of blindness? He or his parents?" Such cold, thoughtless, unsympathetic conversation in the presence of afflicted individuals has caused many such unfortunates to lose courage, give up in despair or disgust, and slink away into seclusion, feeling more helpless than ever. But not this man; he stayed in there.

We occasionally learn of individuals whom we would like to have known, at least by name. Here is one of these, who, though long since departed, can still challenge us with his rare combination of gratitude, unshakable loyalty, and courage of conviction.

Having disposed of their questioning in a firm, but gracious manner, Jesus then resorted to an unusual procedure; instead of healing the blind man immediately, as he had in numerous instances, he coated his eyes with clay, after which he instructed him to make his way to the Pool of Siloam and wash off the clay.

Would it be worthwhile to carry out such a strange instruction? Was this another of those numerous suggestions as to how he might be healed, a remedy to be tried without results? Or was it another of those cheap tricks designed to embarrass him? Or perhaps this was another of those efforts to brush him off, to be rid of him.

Dismal thoughts of this nature might easily have flitted through the poor man's mind as he turned away still blind.

However, faith, courage, and initiative prompted this afflicted man to carry out that simple yet strange instruction with gratifying results—only to find his jubilance quenched by further difficulty; his trouble was by no means over.

When some of his neighbors saw him walking about, they registered various reactions. Some recognized him as the man whom they had frequently seen begging. Others declared that it couldn't be; surely it must be someone who resembled him.

Then some of them began questioning him to learn how his healing had come about. However, they registered less elation over his having gained his sight than curiosity to learn the whereabouts of the one who had healed him.

Then, after learning the identity of his healer, they demanded: "Where is he?" Word had been circulated that anyone who had anything to do with "that man Jesus" was to be turned out of the synagogue.

Now they bring him before those Pharisees who began questioning him as to how and by whom he had been healed.

Although he had not yet seen his Healer, because when he left Jesus and made his way to the Pool of Siloam to wash his eyes, he was still blind; that he knew who his benefactor was is indicated by his response to the Pharisees' question, an answer given them even though he was aware of what the consequences would be.

His neighbors were not the only ones who turned against him. Now the Pharisees call in his parents and begin questioning them as to what they know about his case. Their evasive answer was:

"He's of age; ask him."

Recalling him, they subjected him to further grilling. How could anyone who deliberately disregarded their traditions *possibly* perform such a miracle? *He simply had to be a sinful man.*

His responses were made with bold and withal sound reasoning. How could it be possible for one who was able to perform such a miracle to be a sinner?

Note what he said: "If he is a sinner, I don't know it. One thing I do know, that being blind now I see" (v. 25).

When they persisted, he responded: "I told you once and you didn't listen; why do you want to hear it again? You don't want to be his disciples, do you?"

When they protested that they didn't know whence Jesus had come, he responded: "This is the marvelous thing, that you don't know whence he is, and yet he was able to open my eyes . . . ."

As this man boldly persisted in upholding Jesus as sinless, the Pharisees accused him of that thing which Jesus' disciples had brought up before Jesus healed him. They told this man: "You were born entirely in sin, and are you instructing us?" (v. 34).

And because he dared to talk back and tried to teach them something, they expelled him from the synagogue.

Later, when Jesus found him in the Temple, he inquired of him: "Do you have faith in the Son of God?"

"And who is he, sir, that I may put my trust in him?" Remember, he had not previously *seen* Jesus. And when Jesus identified himself, the man exclaimed: "I have the faith, Lord," and he worshiped him (vv. 36-39).

And now that he had received his sight, in order to be restored to the good graces of the Pharisees like that lame man who had been healed at the Pool of Bethsaida (John 5), he too could have turned against his Healer.

But there was something worthwhile, something noble about this man that prevented his being so ungrateful, so unworthy. Assuredly this man is also one of these anonymous individuals to whom the writer of Hebrews refers. It would be wonderful to know his name.

On the other hand, would it not be even more wonderful and worthwhile for us to profit by his exemplary courage of conviction in the face of such adverse circumstances, his expulsion from the synagogue, in the light of the stigma that this would involve?

He was given the assurance that he would be admitted into the eternal kingdom of God, on the promise given to him by God's own Son, Jesus Christ.

He is among the many who can now look down and cheer us on as we run the race set before us. He is another of those whom we will enjoy meeting when we too go on to be with the Lord.

Touch of Faith

Mark 5:25-35 [1]

When Jesus recrossed the lake after healing the Gerasene demoniac, a large crowd was waiting for him, among them Jairus, whose

47

little daughter was at the point of death. The crowd followed them, among them was a woman who had exhausted her finances paying doctor bills, only to find her condition growing worse instead of better. Hers was indeed a pitiful case.

Had someone who had been healed by the Great Physician described to her the sensation, the satisfaction of being restored to health—immediately and without cost?

Inasmuch as he had healed others, why could he not also heal her, in her pitiful condition? Certainly it was worth trying. Who in similar circumstances would not have joined that multitude following the great Healer?

What was her reaction, however, when she joined that immense throng pressing about him? Surely she must have wavered a bit. How could she, a helpless invalid, expect to attract that great man's attention? How could she even hope to come close to him without being shoved aside or severely injured, perhaps even trampled to death?

Despair, which sometimes leads to desperation and defeat, can also breed new hope and ingenuity. After all, what had she to lose? On the other hand, think of what she might gain! Others had proven this for her.

And so the poor woman exercised amazing faith—notwithstanding a vast degree of timidity and trepidation—also, undoubtedly, modesty, not being willing to attract the attention of so great a throng of people, including the ruler of a synagogue.

That it was timidity and not lack of faith on her part is evidenced by the manner in which she approached the Lord Jesus; she did not confront him or fall at his feet begging for mercy or pity because of her hopeless condition and financial poverty.

"Now if I could just slip up behind him, then reach out and merely touch the hem of his garment . . . " (v. 28).

Herein lies the great difference between individuals; while some have what it takes, others lack it. This woman had it!

Several of the details in this incident merit special consideration, among them Jesus' query as to who had touched him, to which his disciples responded defensively; with so great a crowd pressing upon him, how could they know who touched him? Doubtless many were brushing against him, some merely out of curiosity, others merely for the thrill to be able later to tell somebody about it.

Nevertheless, of all those who could or might have touched him, to our knowledge *only one was healed*. How many impotent people who were there on this occasion could or might have touched him but went away lamenting, "Now why didn't *I* think of that?" "Why is it that nothing like that could happen to me?" "That might have happened to me just as well as to that poor woman."

Since Jesus knew, as he informed the disciples, that power had gone out of him and that the woman had been healed, why was it that he embarrassed this poor woman who displayed so great faith, causing her to tremble as she hesitatingly stepped forward to identify herself? When he asked that question, undoubtedly the crowd fell back, apprehensive lest he should single out one of them—particularly those curiosity seekers—or perhaps someone who was apprehensive lest a hostile Pharisee or Sadducee might be present and cause trouble.

Despite her timidity and embarrassment, despite a possible sense of guilt due to her boldness in touching his garment, aware that Jesus knew her identity, and grateful for the miracle which had taken place within her body, she stepped forward and reverently fell at Jesus' feet while acknowledging that she was the one.

Now, if the Master had actually intended to embarrass this poor woman, then why would he have rewarded her bold faith by healing her? Surely there must have been another reason for his calling special attention to her.

This is substantiated by what the Lord then said to her: "Be cheerful, daughter; your faith has saved you" (Matt. 9:22).

His focusing special attention upon her was undoubtedly designed to impress upon the multitude that had been pressing against him this valuable lesson in exemplary faith—simply reaching out and touching the edge of his garment and being rewarded with that which human beings were incapable of supplying for her.

The message therefore which comes down to us from this unidentified woman of great faith is that God is mindful of our needs. When we reach out to him in simple, sincere trust, he is willing and ready to respond.

Is she not therefore also worthy of special mention and a place of honor in faith's hall of fame?

"Who touched me?" He knows, but he wants us to be conscious

of his knowledge and of his willingness to respond.

[1] And Matthew 9:20-22; Luke 8:43-48.

Cooperation

Matthew 9:1-8; Mark 2:1-12; Luke 5:17-26   *We saw a paradox today.*

"It can't be done. Sorry!"

How frequently have such words been repeated through the ages, when a new project has been proposed, a difficult task suggested, or a seemingly insurmountable obstacle encountered!

In many instances projects have been abandoned and propositions have been rejected altogether without much effort to determine whether some means might possibly be found of making them work.

Something like this could have occurred even before these four men carried this palsied sufferer as far as the house in which Jesus was speaking to a large group of scribes and Pharisees—perhaps, it has been suggested, the home of Simon Peter.

Whether the four were acting on impulse, on the strength of faith, or because of a sincere desire to be helpful or whether the invalid himself, eager to be carried to the Healer, had solicited their assistance and whether difficulty had been encountered in soliciting the services of the four, we can only surmise.

And now, after carrying the poor invalid to the door of that house, they discover that the entrance is blocked by a crowd of dignitaries and curiousity seekers.

"We might have known that something like this would happen." "Oh, what's the use?" "Well, anyway, we tried to do our part." "Well, let's take him back home." "Sorry, my poor friend!"

"Wait a moment; let's not give up. Surely there must be a way to get him inside."

"How?" comes from one of the others, perhaps with a note of sarcasm. "Do you think we can climb up on the roof and—"

"That's a good idea! Let's look for a rope, carry him up there and tear up the roof above where the Healer is standing, then let him down directly in front of him!" The speaker could have been a carpenter or perhaps a thinker or a dreamer.

However that might have come about, inspired by a combination of persistence, ingenuity, and skill, the four carried the man up to the roof, tore up the tile, and lowered him into the room below.

Try to reconstruct in your mind's eye the picture of this quartet standing up there on that roof, peering down through that hole at those startled dignitaries, Pharisees, and teachers of the law from Galilee, Judea, and Jerusalem. What will their reaction be when they discover who is responsible for so strange and daring an intrusion?

Now comes another moment of suspense. What will be the reaction of the great Teacher? Now he has spoken, but the spirit of those dignitaries must not be favorable, for he is rebuking them—something about the forgiveness of sin.

Isn't he going to heal the poor fellow after all? Will he go on preaching to that crowd? Of what benefit will that be to this poor, sick man lying there at his feet? It is probably upsetting the poor fellow all the more, especially after all that he has already suffered. How long will this go on? Now those dignitaries are arguing with him. What next?

Now they hear the Teacher ordering their friend to get to his feet, to pick up that couch on which the four of them had brought him, and to carry it home! Here comes another moment of suspense.

It is once again impossible to imagine the reaction of these four as they stand up there on that roof and see the man get to his feet, pick up his couch, and make his way through that crowd and out of the house—under his own power!

The four undoubtedly sought to avoid those hostile, disgruntled Pharisees, who had surely glanced up and caught a glimpse of them standing there about that opening which they had made. Yet surely they hurried down to share the joy of him in whose miraculous recovery they had so important a part.

What a marvelous message these four can even now convey to posterity, that what one individual is unable to undertake alone can be accomplished with the cooperation of others, all working together.

Foreigner's Faith

Matthew 8:5-13; Luke 7:1-10   Just say the word, and . . . .

There are situations from which we confidently anticipate favorable results. But what a surprise, what a letdown when those anticipated results do not materialize!

There are, on the other hand, situations out of which we are certain that little or nothing will develop. What a delightful surprise when the unexpected does take place!

Here is a man, not an Israelite, but a centurian in the Roman army of occupation for which the Israelites had little respect. This man, however, was different; he was highly respected. He had even provided for them a synagogue in which they could worship.

The accounts in Matthew and Luke differ somewhat as to details. Although Matthew records that the man approached Jesus personally, Luke records that Jewish leaders were the first to contact Jesus, then his servants. However, this is not necessarily a discrepancy or contradiction. On the contrary, Luke has provided more of the details. In those days, as in ours, it was not unusual for someone in a position of authority to act, not in person, but through those under his authority. This is brought out in a statement which he made to Jesus: "I have men under me . . . . "

There might have been several reasons for his not coming to Jesus in person, one of which was his modesty or his sense of unworthiness (Luke 7:6), another might have been his concern for the sick boy and his desire to remain close by.

Other Roman soldiers had solicited the Messiah's help, for example Jairus who implored him to accompany him to his home to heal his daughter who was at the point of death (Luke 8:41-42). This unnamed centurion, however, not only displayed remarkable faith but also displayed remarkable reasoning ability and compassion.

I also am a man under authority, having soldiers under me, and I tell this one, 'Go,' and he goes, and to another, 'Come,' and he comes, and to my servant, 'Do this,' and he does it."

He was not trying to exercise his military authority by ordering the Master to go over and heal the boy. On the contrary, when Jesus volunteered to go, and had actually started, as Luke records, the centurion said: "That will not be necessary. I'm not even worthy to have you enter my house. All you need to do is to say the word and the boy will be healed."

Notice also: the boy was not his own son, but a slave boy. When the slave became ill, the centurion might well have decided: "Why should I trouble that Healer by asking him to come over here to heal that boy? I can pick up another slave right here whenever I desire."

Here indeed is a rare combination of reasoning, faith, concern, and compassion. Is it any wonder then that the Lord Jesus responded in a manner seldom reported of him—"marvelled" at this man's unusual demonstration of faith? And where in Scripture is greater faith than this to be found?

Jairus, an Israelite, did not insist that the Master need not accompany him to his home to heal his dying daughter, but insisted that he hurry before it was too late. And although that Syrophoenician woman begged Jesus to accompany her to her home to heal her daughter, her faith was not nearly as strong as was this Roman centurion's. Jesus sent her home with the assurance that the girl would be well.

It would be well to recall in this connection that Jesus did not always deal with people in the same manner, but rather he dealt with them according to their faith, as individuals.

All that we know about this unusual Roman soldier is contained in these two parallel accounts in Matthew and Luke. Nevertheless, even though we are unable to identify him by name, he presents a challenging example and message to many of us today, who are too frequently numbered among those to whom Jesus frequently exclaimed: "O you of little faith!"

Can you not also hear the Master challenging us with those familiar words: "You go and do likewise"? Or perhaps these: "When the Son of man comes, will he find faith upon the earth?"

The consideration of this incident in connection with the case of a nobleman who came to Cana and implored Jesus to come with him to Capernaum to heal his dying son will serve as an interesting study in contrast (John 4:46-54).

Intruder

Matthew 15:21-28; Mark 7:24-30

In order to be alone with his disciples and give them private instructions, the Lord Jesus withdrew with them to Tyre and Sidon, away from the crowds that were following him and from those hostile Jewish leaders who were persistently heckling him.

As this was to be a rest period, a vacation, he did not want their presence to be known. Nevertheless in some way word got out; a woman who learned that he was there came to ask of him a favor.

Perturbed by her presence and her persistence, the disciples urged the Lord to send her away. Doubtless they themselves had endeavored to be rid of her but without success.

From the disciples' viewpoint, there was another reason for chasing her away. Tyre and Sidon was foreign territory. Besides, she was a Greek, a Gentile. Still another point which, in the eyes of a loyal Jew, would militate against this persistent woman is introduced by Matthew (15:22); she was a Canaanitess, descendant of people who, failing to measure up to God's expectation of a nation, were to be replaced by his chosen people, Israel.

At least ostensibly in keeping with the disciples' attempt to be rid of her, the Lord introduced yet another logical reason for turning her away: "I was not sent out except to the lost sheep of the house of Israel" (Matt. 15:24).

Still she persisted not with a hostile or defiant attitude but rather with fervent earnestness: "Lord, help me."

Now Jesus gives her an answer that would have turned off and sent away many individuals in a rage: "First permit the children to be fed, for it is not good to take the children's bread and throw it down to the little puppies" (Mark 7:27).

Even this did not deter this woman's determination to get what she had come to seek. Undoubtedly recognizing the Jewish attitude toward foreigners, which might have discouraged even irritated many others, she responded with remarkable cleverness: "Yes, Lord, and those little puppies under the table eat of the crumbs of the children!"

That did it! Commending her for such great faith, Jesus assured her that her petition was being granted. And returning home she found her daughter up and around, completely recovered.

What a wonderful testimony this foreign woman has left us. Many now, like many of those who followed Jesus then, can be put to shame by the Master's exclamation: "O you of little faith!" She was a foreigner and a descendant of those whose land the Hebrews had possessed. She came at so inauspicious a time and was then informed that the Lord had come primarily to the house of Israel. Lastly, she was compared with a little puppy under the table—nevertheless, she stayed in there till she received, not an outburst of impatient, indignant rebuke, but Jesus' warm commendation and the assurance that what she had requested was granted.

The incident also drives home this truth: Bold persistence is not limited to those of us who consider ourselves the elect of God. Unfortunately, those from whom such a bold display of faith might be expected is not always forthcoming.

It would not be out of order to add this footnote: Often when so marvelous a display of faith comes from so unexpected a source, those who count themselves the elect are not too well pleased. In some cases they are inclined to be resentful and unmindful that such an individual's subsequent joy over victory and the manifestation of God's grace and mercy may mean much more to that "outsider" than it means to them.

Those "outsiders" frequently put to shame many whose privileged position should inspire them to become gleaming examples instead of jealous or skeptical critics.

Royalty's Reward

John 4:46-54   Proceed, your son is alive.

The news of Jesus' miracles was spreading so rapidly that when he returned from Samaria to Cana of Galilee, where he had performed that first miracle, crowds came from all around bringing their sick and afflicted.

From Capernaum came a nobleman, an officer in the service of

King Herod Antipas. He came not out of curiosity nor because he had faith in Jesus as the promised Messiah; he had a son at the point of death back home and wanted to bring the Healer back with him to spare the boy's life.

"Unless you (plural) see signs and wonders, you will not have faith," was Jesus' response (v. 48). (It is possible that he put this in the form of a question, "Will you not have faith?")

Jesus did not grant the nobleman's request. Instead, in his gracious manner he told him: "Proceed, your child is alive."

That his response had its effect upon the man is indicated by the fact that he turned away and proceeded to return home.

In this incident we observe one of those marvelously meaningful methods which Jesus employed in dealing with individuals. Instead of granting their requests outright, he responded in a manner designed to make them aware of his supreme power and greatness—not merely as a great healer or miracle worker but as the Son of the supreme God. Jesus lived in keeping with his primary purpose for coming into the world—to bring sinful, disobedient human beings to a true knowledge of and a relationship with God, his heavenly Father.

That the man's request was purely selfish is indicated by his urgent response: "Sir, come on down before my child dies." Had he expected Jesus to accompany him, stand over his son, and, speaking magic words, have the boy be healed and suddenly stand up—perhaps for the prestige it might bring to the nobleman?

What were that father's reactions as he turned away? Was he disappointed, perhaps disgruntled, because the Healer disregarded his official prestige? Was he wondering how those back home were going to react? And as he proceeded was he wondering whether on reaching his home he was actually going to find the boy alive or dead?

That he waited till the following day to return home is not necessarily an indication of his faith in Jesus' response. The hour was late, and night travel in those days was unsafe.

John does inform us that as the nobleman turned away, he did manifest a degree of faith in Jesus' assurance. The Lord was not only putting him to a test but was also demonstrating to him his divine ability to heal at so great a distance.

What were his reactions on the way home the following day when glancing down the road he saw approaching, perhaps at a rapid speed, several of his servants? What news were they bringing, good or bad? This was undoubtedly a very tense moment.

His first question, after hearing the good news, was: "What time was it when he began recovering?"

"The fever left him at the seventh hour."

That was the very time, he recognized, at which Jesus had assured him: " . . . Your son is alive" (v. 53).

What sort of message would you expect this Roman officer to convey to us today? "When I learned about this great Healer, I wanted to bring him over here to heal my son, and so I went over there intending to bring him back here with me. I had no idea that he could do it this way! But when they came and told me that the boy was healed at that very hour, that was sufficient for me and for my family. We all knew that we could put our trust in him."

Suppose that the miracle had been performed as the Roman officer had anticipated. Like many others, nine of those ten lepers for example, he too might have gone his merry way, admitting that a miracle had been performed but failing to appreciate fully the divine power of Jesus. And he and his family might not have placed their trust in the Lord as the Son of the living God.

He can convey a greatly needed message to many in our day who are looking to God for spectacular bodily healing but seemingly manifest little if any interest in the great truth of which the Savior manifested great concern. Jesus was not merely commissioned for the healing of their human bodies. He came to redeem their immortal souls with a love and a compassion that culminated in his offering his own life that they might live—eternally.

What, we may ask further, became of this Roman nobleman, his son whose life was thus prolonged, and the other members of his family? Did they also melt into that great host that failed to follow Jesus? Was their faith, like that of so many, merely temporal? Or did they bear witness among those with whom they came in contact? This we do not know, nor do we even know their identity, except that he had some sort of royal connection.

What testimonies he and his family could have given, had they too, like many of whom we read in Scripture, joined those who followed Jesus to the very end! This, too, can be that royal man's

57

contribution to those of our day, unless, of course, they were numbered among the multitude who did follow Jesus. But this, unfortunately, we do not know.

Disgruntled Disinherited

Luke 12:13 ff.

"Man, who appointed me a judge or a divider over you?"

Here we find undoubtedly Jesus' most emphatic refusal to grant
an individual's request recorded in any of the Gospels. The man,
one of the multitude following Jesus, had asked: "Teacher, tell my
brother to share the inheritance with me."

We do not know the circumstances involved in this case, whether
for one reason or another the father had disinherited him or whether
the brother had deliberately confiscated the entire inheritance, legally
or otherwise.

We can reasonably infer, however, on the basis of Jesus' response
that the man's motive was selfish—and certainly not in keeping with
the purpose for which the Lord Jesus had descended to this earth.

The disinherited man's request prompted Jesus to speak that pun-
gent parable of a farmer whose land yielded a bumper crop. Sitting
down, he had a conference with himself and came up with the decision
to replace his barns with larger ones, shore up that big crop, then
start "living it up."

Actually we have here two unnamed individuals, for the Master
has introduced this parable with a narrative statement: "A certain
wealthy man's land produced an abundant crop" (v. 16).

And this was one of those rare occasions on which God called a
man a "fool." [1] In making his decision, that selfish, unwise farmer
had failed to recognize or take into account his Creator who had
the power over both life and death. "This night they shall demand
of you your life (soul); and what you have stored up, whose will
they be?"

Whether this frustrated brother remained to listen to Jesus' parable
we are not informed; Jesus, according to Luke's account, spoke this
parable "to them," those who did remain, many of whom undoubt-

edly needed it as much as did this disinherited man.

If he had tarried even a little longer, he would also have heard the Master speak to his disciples about the value of storing up a heritage, not merely for this life, but for the life to come, where neither fellow heir or anyone or anything else can take it away. He would have heard of the inability of Solomon with all of his wealth and wisdom to adorn himself as God does perishable grass and lilies. Hence God could and would also see that man's temporary abode and other needs were adequately provided for; and what is more, God does not desire humans to miss out on the opportunities here on earth of making provision for man's *inner* self which will outlive his outer being.

This is the way God planned it and the way God wants and encourages us to permit it to be.

And this is the urgent message that can come out of the long ago from this disgruntled, disinherited brother who, long since has gone to his eternal destiny (wherever that may be in his case).

This man's counsel, also the counsel of that foolish farmer, can still be: "Don't make the same tragic mistake that I made, by placing emphasis on the wrong thing."

[1] Greek *aphron,* "senseless, foolish, unwise."

Defiant Steward

Luke 19:11-27 From your own mouth I judge you.

Though the nobleman in this parable had an experience similar to that of a man named Archelaus who went to Rome to request the emperor to appoint him king of his province, Jesus has not identified this man by name.

Before leaving, this man entrusted to each of his ten servants a sum of money [1] with instructions that they invest the money for him during his absence.

On his return he called in the ten for an accounting, rewarding each, not only with what he had earned from his investment, but also with the money which he had given him—with one exception.

The tenth servant returned only what had been given to him with the explanation that he had not invested it because he considered his master a selfish, dishonest man.

The master's response has been interpreted, not as an admission of the truth of that accusation, but rather as either an exclamation of sarcasm, or a question: "You knew that I am an austere man, taking up what I did not put down, and reaping what I did not sow?" (vv. 22 f.).

By refusing to invest that money, this servant was hurting, not his landlord, but himself. Not only did he lose whatever he might have gained by investing his master's money, but that which he had been given to invest was also taken away from him and given to the servant who had earned the greatest amount.

This nobleman who had become a king did not need that which his servants had earned, did not in fact need even that which he had given those servants to invest; if the money had been a necessity, he would certainly have accepted it instead of giving it all to them.

This parable was directed especially against those hostile Israelites in Jerusalem who were rejecting him and clamoring for his execution. It applies equally, however, to all human beings who in like manner reject Jesus and what his heavenly Father through him has made available to them, including of course eternal salvation.

They who fail or refuse to exercise the faith necessary to obtain this eternal salvation for which Jesus has paid so tremendous a price (when the Holy Spirit offers it to them), and those who, like this belligerent, obstinate servant, accuse God of being unfair, unjust, selfish, and interested only in his own advantage, can expect the same treatment accorded this rebellious servant.

To carry this parallel farther, God does not need anything from his mortal creatures, for all that exists belongs to him by right of creation and has been placed at our disposal by him. Failure to respond to his will, as in the case of this rebellious servant, results in cheating oneself, not God.

One might even go farther and declare that God does not even need our feeble expressions of gratitude and praise, but here again, by withholding such expressions, we do more harm to ourselves than we do to God. And whatever we do for God is not to our own glory but to his glory and praise in appreciation for all that he has done for us.

This meaningful parable also furnishes enlightenment to two currently discussed topics, one of which is: "Who crucified Jesus?" And the answer is that they who reject Jesus as the Author and the Finisher of our salvation "crucify him again for themselves and put him to shame" (Heb. 6:6).

The second is: "God is too good to send anyone to hell."

This is substantiated by God's marvelous grace. In sending his own Son into this world to take our place in death, we are enabled to occupy that place which he has made possible for those of us who put our trust in him and who avail ourselves of the salvation which he has made possible at so tremendous a price, not to us, but to himself.

[1] A mina (Greek, *MNA*).

Among So Many

John 6:1-13

All four Gospels contain this familiar story. However, John has included several details which add to the interest.

He informs us that late in the afternoon when Jesus asked Philip where they would find food for that weary multitude out there in that desolate place, Philip replied that the two hundred denarii which they had in the treasury was not enough to buy food for so great a number of people (John 6:7).

John is also the writer who informs us that the meager lunch used to feed those five thousand was furnished by a little boy, perhaps a slave boy,[1] and that Andrew, the quieter of those two brothers, was the one who informed Jesus about this boy.

Whether Andrew brought this boy to Jesus, or whether he took his lunch from him and brought it, we are not informed. Andrew was either hesitant or skeptical, perhaps both, as is indicated by his guarded comment: "But what are these among so many?"

Nevertheless, since this was the only food available in that desolate place, under the circumstances it had to be this or nothing at all!

From that point on no further mention is made of this boy.

Since he was a mere obscure peasant boy, perhaps a runaway

slave who followed Jesus merely out of curiosity, perhaps to see what sort of miracle would be performed next, what can be gained by spending any more time on him?

It is not difficult to imagine what a lasting impression so spectacular an event as this would make on a growing boy, as was true in the case of that youth in whose house Jesus ate that last Passover with his disciples and instituted that first Memorial Supper. That night the youth slipped out in his nightgown and followed Jesus and the disciples, but in his effort to escape when Jesus was apprehended, he lost that garment and ran home without it, as years later he recorded in his Gospel (see Mark 14:50-52).

"Just think! That great Teacher took my little lunch—those five little barley loaves and two bits of fish—hardly enough to keep *me* from starving—and fed that big crowd of five thousand or more men!

"They reminded me of flower beds, sitting out there in groups of about fifty each on that green grass, dressed in their different-colored clothes!

"And that wasn't all! When everybody had as much as they could eat, the Teacher sent those twelve men out to gather up the leftovers, and when they came back they had a lot more than what he had when he sent them out—twelve whole baskets full of those pieces of barley bread!"

Try now to visualize the possibilities presented to this lad whose curiosity and initiative had prompted him to follow that big crowd, the testimony he could have given to many others!

But wait: Did he share it with others? Or did circumstances cause him to hesitate to share this wonderful experience with anyone else— perhaps the fear of being punished by his parents for running away or by his master if he was a slave boy? Or was he perhaps afraid of what those hostile Jewish leaders might do to him for having followed Jesus?

This calls to mind a comment heard quite frequently these days: "If I had lived back there and heard Jesus and witnessed some of those miracles, I might have believed in him . . ."

Here is the account of a lad who both heard and saw Jesus and witnessed one of his best-known miracles—in fact, had an important part in that incident. Did that cause him to become a follower of

Jesus and to place his faith in him as the Son of the living God? If so, we can find no record of it.

This event has obviously made a much greater and more vivid impression upon posterity than upon this so highly favored boy. Was it then a golden opportunity lost—or did the lad continue to follow the great Miracle Worker? Eternity alone will reveal.

Someone has ventured the hope that the boy had been given one of those twelve baskets of bread collected by the disciples. Would this not have fallen far, far short of what he could have gained from so phenomenal an experience?

In view of current questioning in certain quarters as to the purpose of Jesus' miracles, further observations are pertinent.

A man whom Jesus healed reminded the rulers of a synagogue: "No one has ever previously opened the eyes of the blind" (John 9).

One winter day in Jerusalem, Israelites came and asked Jesus: "How long will you keep our souls up in the air . . . ?"

"The works which I perform in the name of my Father," Jesus responded, *"these* testify concerning me" (John 10:25).

He performed these miracles, not merely to meet human needs, important as that was, but to demonstrate the power and authority which he himself had as the Son of the living God.

This was graphically demonstrated to this poor boy, from whom we can learn, not merely what *might* have been if he had taken advantage of his wonderful opportunity, but what *can be in our case.*

As Jesus told Thomas a week after his resurrection: "Happy are they who, not having seen, nevertheless have faith" (John 20:29).

Now, what was the effect of this miracle upon the five thousand who partook of the boy's meager lunch? He must be their Promised Messiah; they tried to seize him and make him their king. Jesus, knowing their intention, slipped away. His was not an earthly but a heavenly kingdom.

And this is another vitally important lesson to be learned from this well-known miracle performed by Jesus. He came not merely to furnish bread for this life but to become the Bread of *eternal* life.

[1] *Paidarion,* a young boy, perhaps a slave, the word Jesus used of children playing in a marketplace (Matt. 11:16).

Child Play

Matthew 11:15-19   We fluted . . . we mourned for you, but you would not.

Most, if indeed not all, of the things which children do when playing are imitations of the things which they observe their elders doing and saying. Elders are often amazed and sometimes shocked and embarrassed by what they observe; for growing children are not always discriminative in their choice of the things which they reproduce or mimic.

The Lord Jesus has left for us this simple, but nonetheless powerful, illustration of children at play in a marketplace imitating their elders.

Several of them were trying to "start something." First they imitated someone playing the flute, but there was no response on the part of their playmates. Then they started playing funeral; still their playmates sat there without responding.

By this time they were disgusted and distressed and sat down. "We played the flute, but you wouldn't get up and respond. Then we played funeral, but you wouldn't mourn. What's wrong with you?"

However, notice this. Instead of telling the people that the children are imitating *them,* Jesus is actually saying in effect: "You adults are acting just like children" (see v. 16). And perhaps as he was speaking they might have been able to hear the children's voices as they were playing in a nearby marketplace.

Jesus had been reminding them of the coming of John the Baptist to prepare the way for his appearance; however, they had reacted just like those children out there who refused to respond.

"And now that I have made my appearance," he reminds them, "you people are refusing to listen to me. You criticized John for one reason, and now you are criticizing me for the opposite reason." They were even going so far as to accuse him of being in league with the devil.

However, unlike those children, the Lord Jesus was not trying to play with them—he meant business. It is going to be more tolerable in the judgment, he informs them, for such cities as Sodom and Gomorrah, Tyre and Sidon than for those who had listened to John the Baptist and who were now listening to Jesus himself but were acting just like those indifferent little children over there—yes, even worse; for now they were seeking for valid excuses for doing away with him.

Later, you will recall, after Jesus came riding into Jerusalem on that colt, and people followed him into the Temple praising him, how children raised their voices and cried out, "Hosanna to the Son of David." The chief priests and the scribes came to Jesus and yelled indignantly: "Don't you hear what they are saying?"

Jesus replied: "Did you never read, 'Out of the mouth of babes and sucklings thou hast perfected praise'?" (see Ps. 8:2).

These children who failed to get a response from their playmates, and those who later brought upon themselves the disfavor and the wrath of their elders who should have known better, and should have listened to them and heeded their message, can still send a valuable demonstration to the heedless multitudes of our own contemporaries: "Why don't you listen and respond?"

A somber note should also be added to their message. Well might they have been saying to posterity: "Did it occur to you that we might have been singing *your* funeral dirge back there?"

First Things First

Luke 9:57-62   First permit me to . . . .

Here at the tip end of Luke 9 is the account of several men who expressed their intention to follow Jesus. He informed one of them that unlike foxes and birds he had no permanent earthly dwelling (v. 58); nothing further is mentioned concerning the man.

He invited another to follow him, and the man replied: "Permit me first to go away to bury my father."

Jesus' response was: "Let the dead bury their own dead; but you, going out, proclaim the Kingdom of God" (v. 60).

If this has a ring of harshness or lack of sympathy, it should be pointed out that if the man's father had been dead at that time, he would not have been there with Jesus but would have been at home, at least until after the father's burial. He was speaking of an indefinite period of time. In those days it was not uncommon for a son to remain close to or in touch with home until after the death of his father.

Think of how much is involved in a decision of this nature, an entirely new life pattern with new emphases, new objectives, not merely for this life but beyond—their eternal destiny.

We have no further record of the subsequent activities of any of these men who turned back. However, they are representative of a considerable segment of society, not only of their own era but of any, including our own.

Under emotional stress, doubtless with sincere conviction, they express a desire or intention to follow Jesus, perhaps even to assume responsibility of some sort in his kingdom work. Nevertheless, they are not quite ready or willing to break away from something or other that stands in their way or holds them back. They intend to do it *some* time but *not just now.*

Knowledge of contemporary cases of this nature, however, warrants the conclusion that their deferred decisions to follow Jesus by no means terminated the matter so far as they were concerned.

Here certainly is evidence that challenges the assertion that it is easy to become a follower of the Lord Jesus Christ. Although Jesus himself is always willing and ready, and the Holy Spirit seeks to convince the individual of his need of salvation, the tempter nevertheless, is still on the job, seeking to place obstacles in the sinner's way.

Sooner or later, somewhere along the way, these procrastinating individuals are confronted with the awareness that they have been missing something of vital importance, and, in many instances if not in all, that something missed has taken a vitally heavy toll from that person's subsequent living. In how many instances this is true we have no accurate means of knowing, for not everyone is willing to permit this be known. In some instances there comes the conviction that now it is too late.

A sculptor has portrayed opportunity as a beautiful woman with a prominent forelock which can be grasped as she approaches. When she has passed by, however, it is discovered that the back of her head is bald, rendering it impossible to grasp and detain her.

There are, to be sure, instances in which regret or remorse impels one to seek to revive that desire to follow and do the will of Jesus. Even in such cases, especially when the procrastination is prolonged, it is difficult, and costly, if indeed possible, to take up where one had left off.

In some instances there may even be a second turning back, leaving a deeper scar. Nor does this end the matter. Individuals have been known to become "all mixed up," and this causes difficulty, not only for the guilty party but also for others whom that individual might have been able to influence; but now it may be too late, for by this time one's influence is likely to be not only negative but possibly adverse.

There are also cases in which these individuals have become so deeply involved in temporal affairs that this new life in Christ Jesus has become more remote than ever.

The message coming from these who said "But first let me . . ." can be summed up in these ominous words: "Don't make the mistake that I made."

Sad indeed are the words: "If I had only . . . !"

Salvation is too wonderfully significant to be disregarded or postponed for the sake of mere temporal interests.

Preoccupied

Luke 14:15-24   I ask you, have me excused.

On one occasion when Jesus was the invited guest of a Pharisee, he observed how the VIPs were pushing and shoving to occupy the most honorable places about the table.

It should be noted, however, that not one of those celebrities is mentioned by name, not even the host himself.

While Jesus was observing them, they were watching him to catch him in something that he might do or say.

During the conversation one of the guests remarked: "Happy is one who eats bread in the kingdom of God." With what intention he spoke or with what degree of sincerity, whether to favorably impress Jesus or to let it be known that he intended to be one of them, or whether he was seeking to involve Jesus in a controversy of some sort, we are not informed.

The man's remark gave Jesus the opportunity of directing the conversation into a fruitful channel, as he did on so many occasions. He told of a man who sent out invitations to attend a great feast and, according to the custom, sent his servants out to inform the invited guests that the feast was ready for them to "come and get it."

Three of those invited guests sent word that they were unable to attend. One needed to go and inspect a piece of land which he had purchased. Another had bought five yoke of oxen and needed to go and try them out. A third man had no excuse—he had a reason; he had married a wife!

Land was needed to grow crops, raise cattle, produce food. Oxen were needed to plough the land and do other essential work. And since the beginning of time men have married wives, established homes, and maintained family life to perpetuate the human race.

However, there is something that needs to be pointed out with reference to these particular excuses.

Anyone who would purchase a piece of land without first looking it over, anyone who would purchase five yoke of oxen without first trying them out, would be displaying immature judgment, in fact actually taking a big risk. What is more, men who have married wives have been known to keep important social engagements.

Those Pharisees to whom Jesus was addressing this parable were deeply involved and engrossed in their own temporal affairs, observing their legal traditions, displaying their self-righteousness (as in this instance competing for the seats of honor at feasts, v. 7). They were too involved in their own affairs of this temporal earthly life to be concerned about eating bread or obtaining any place at all in the eternal kingdom of God.

It would be well also to remind ourselves that what Jesus is portraying and impressing upon the minds and hearts, not only of that group of self-satisfied Pharisees but upon all of us as well, is that many of these earthly activities that seem to mean so much to us are not to be compared with that wonderful privilege of eating bread in the kingdom of God. Being so engrossed in these temporal activities will prove futile in comparison with the acceptance of the invitation to be present at the eternal love feast which God, through his Son Jesus Christ, has prepared for us at so tremendous a price—the sacrifice of his Son as the Lamb of God and the Bread of life, *eternal* life.

Ominous Obstacle

Mark 10:17-31 [1]   *One thing you lack . . . .*

We learn several things about this man: He was young (Matt. 19:22), a ruler, in a position of authority (Luke 18:18), very wealthy (Matt. 19:22; Mark 10:22; Luke 18:23), that Jesus loved him (Mark 10:21), that he was undoubtedly of good moral character (Matt. 19:20; Mark 10:20; Luke 18:21), eager and energetic (Mark 10:17), and an unusually outstanding young man.

Apart from this his identity is purely a matter of speculation. As for the theory that he might have been Saul of Tarsus, certainly he who admitted that he had guarded the garments of those who had stoned Stephen and had severely persecuted the early Christians would not be likely to withhold the information that on one occasion he had seen and talked with the Lord Jesus.

Although this is one of the more familiar incidents in the ministry of Jesus, there are several things involved here that may not be so familiar to many of us.

He and the Master were agreed on one point; despite his commendable qualities, yet *he lacked one thing*. As to the nature of that one thing, however, they did not agree.

The young man approached Jesus eagerly (running, Mark informs us, 10:17), desiring to learn how he might have eternal life. But careful examination of their conversation reveals quite clearly that the young man was not thinking of everlasting life in terms of what Jesus was teaching.

Note carefully now the Commandments which Jesus mentions to him, and which he says he has always been observing (the Fifth through the Ninth).

In neither of the three Gospels in which their conversation is recorded is the Tenth Commandment mentioned: "You shall not covet . . . ." This was actually the one thing that prompted this promising young man to turn away sorrowfully in his unwillingness to dispose of his wealth. He would have been in a position to learn the way of everlasting life—to come back and follow Jesus.

This actually suggests two possibilities. He was hoping to be able to buy his way into eternity or to be permitted to enjoy his wealth for a longer time here on earth, perhaps forever.

Perhaps he was not certain in his own thinking which it might be, just so long as he would be able to enjoy those possessions forever.

What the Lord Jesus said to him further obviously substantiates this: he told him to distribute his wealth to the poor and to the needy, then he would have treasures awaiting him in heaven. Then Jesus added, "And come and follow me."

Note further that among the five Commandments which Jesus did *not* quote to him are the first four, which pertain to one's relationship with God. That he was leaving God out of his thinking, planning, and living—except in seeking what God might provide as a means of his enjoying for a longer time what he already possessed—is revealed by his reaction to Jesus' admonition: "He went away sorrowful."

If he had been interested in seeking God's will and concerned about pleasing God, surely he would not have turned away refusing to take that first step toward securing eternal life and, incidentally, having treasure laid up for him in heaven.

Here again all three Gospels record his reason for turning away. This is reinforced by what Jesus said after the young man departed. What Jesus said puzzled not only his disciples but also many people since then. It would be easier, Jesus declared, for a camel to pass through a needle's eye than for a man of wealth to enter the kingdom of heaven.

Whether Jesus intended this to be a figure of hyperbole with a touch of humor, as many interpret it or whether, as has also been suggested, Jesus was referring to a mountain passage not far away known as Needle's Eye through which it was impossible for a camel to pass without the removal of whatever burden it carried, the application is the same: It is impossible to transport material possessions into spiritual heaven.

Was it the young man's wealth itself that kept him out of the kingdom of heaven? We have no record that anyone told Barnabas to part with his wealth before becoming a Christian. What, then, is the difference? He did not allow his wealth to keep him out of the kingdom; instead, he used what he possessed as a means of his increased usefulness. He voluntarily laid at the feet of the apostles the entire proceeds from the sale of a piece of property. For a time he did missionary work with the apostle Paul and then went out on his own reclaiming John Mark who became a valuable servant of the Lord Jesus.

As for the wealth which this young ruler ultimately left behind, we might ask the question which God asked of a prosperous farmer who decided to build bigger barns to store up his bumper crop and take life easy. God told him that his time had come to leave the earth, and asked him: "Then whose shall these things be which you have stored up?" (Luke 12:20).

The most valuable heritage which this wealthy young ruler left to posterity is his well-known rejection of Jesus' challenge, which would have brought him something vastly more valuable than what he obviously came seeking so earnestly, eternal *spiritual* life, with treasure which not even death itself could have taken from him.

1 Matthew 19:16 to 20:16; Luke 18:18-30.

Not Far—How Near?

Mark 12:28-34 [1]   *You are not far from the Kingdom of God.*

While the Pharisees were gloating over the humiliation of a Sadducee who had tried to trap Jesus (Matt. 22:23-33), this pharisaical lawyer, recognizing that Jesus had answered that Sadducee "well," stepped forward and tempted Jesus with this question:

"Teacher, which is the great commandment in the law?"

Jesus responded by quoting two Commandments that dealt with one's attitude toward both God and one's fellowmen. "On these two commandments," he added, "hang the whole law and the prophets" (Matt. 22:40).

The lawyer agreed that these were the greatest commandments, greater even than burnt offerings and sacrifices (Mark 12:32-34).

Knowing that he had answered with a degree of sincerity, Jesus informed him: "You are not far from the Kingdom of God" (v. 34).

Then since this scribe was so close to the kingdom, why was it that Jesus did not encourage him to take that final step? Had not another member of his party, a ruler, called upon Jesus one night, acknowledging that one who could do what Jesus was doing must certainly be of God? (John 3:2). Would not another Pharisee, recognized as an outstanding teacher, caution the Sanhedrin to be careful how they dealt with Jesus' followers lest they act in opposition to the will of God? (Acts 5:34 ff.). And would Jesus not stop one of the teacher's followers (Saul) who was on his way to Damascus with permission to apprehend followers of Jesus? (Acts 9).

But who, after all, makes the final decision for the individual?

The answer is actually two-fold. God provides the means, and he gives the opportunity. The response depends not upon God's willingness to accept him, which God has already manifested, but upon the individual. Our opinions, our sentiments have absolutely nothing to do with the individual's final response or failure to respond. And in view of everything which God through his Son Jesus has done to make his eternal kingdom accessible, what right or what authority have we to question or blame God?

Was it not selfishness or covetousness, for example, that prevented that wealthy young ruler from obtaining eternal life? And in the light of what Jesus told Nicodemus, without regeneration from above there would be no possibility of even seeing the kingdom of God. If Nicodemus had expressed the desire to experience that rebirth, it would then have been made available to him. But we can find no record of his having been born from above.

What was it that hindered this Pharisee from coming all the way?

The answer is to be found in his response to what Jesus said to him: "You really told the truth, Teacher, when you said that God is one and that apart from him there is no other" (Mark 12:32).

Like multitudes of his fellow Israelites, this scribe was not willing to concede that Jesus was the Son of God; to him this would be tantamount to Jesus' exalting himself to a position equal to God himself, which, you will recall, was the strongest argument used by the Sadducees and Pharisees—undoubtedly including this scribe himself—in demanding that Pontius Pilate have Jesus crucified (see John 19:7).

This scribe, along with other Israelites, was not only brushing aside those many Old Testament prophesies concerning the coming of God's own Son into the world; he was also disregarding the fact that one of the words for God in the Old Testament is *Elohim,* which is plural.

If this man had become a follower of Jesus, he might even have heard God the Father himself audibly claim Jesus as his only begotten Son (Matt. 3:17; 17:5; Mark 1:11).

It is generally accepted that "a miss is as good as a mile." Many a race, many a contest has been *nearly* won, many a goal or objective *almost* reached. Nevertheless, out of his great grace, mercy, and loving-kindness God is expected by many to ignore this axiom, even though an individual has been unwilling to accept what God has provided (and at so great a price)—the crucifixion of his own Son, Jesus Christ.

Finite minds find it difficult or impossible to comprehend the profoundly wonderful fact of the triune God—the Father, Son, and Holy Spirit. However, in light of what Jesus said to his disciples on the eve of his crucifixion, "if it were not so, I would have told you" (John 14:2)—which can be interpreted as meaning, "I wouldn't deliberately deceive or lie to you"—those of us who exercise the faith find the Holy Spirit ready to reveal this great and profound truth.

They are Three, yet, as Jesus has assured us, there is no conflict but only complete unity and harmony between the Father, the Son, and the Holy Spirit. And as someone has wonderfully expressed it, the great love of God begins right there in the Trinity.

This legalistic Pharisee, who was so positive that he would succeed in exposing Jesus when others had failed, has actually left to posterity something worthy of serious consideration. Something which prevented him from entering the kingdom but can assist others in avoiding the mistake which he made is that of permitting their preconceived notions and opinions to hinder them from yielding to the convincing, convicting power of the Holy Spirit who was sent into the world to make available the kingdom which God the Father sent his only begotten Son into the world to make possible to mankind by sacrificing his own life. The kingdom was made available from which this scribe was just far enough away to be unwilling and unable to enter, despite Jesus' encouragement: "You are not far . . . ."

[1] Also Matthew 22: 34-40.

Compassionate Father

Luke 15:11-32

In responding to the Pharisees and Sadducees who criticized him for associating and eating with tax collectors and sinners, Jesus spoke three parables. He introduced the first of these by saying: "What man of you . . . ?" (v. 4), the second with "what woman . . . ?" (v. 8). These of course could refer to anyone who might act as they would.

He introduces as a narrative: "A certain man had two sons" (v. 11). It would therefore be within reason to conclude that Jesus was recounting an actual experience. Inasmuch as this story is used or referred to by many speakers, teachers, and preachers, wouldn't it be interesting to be able to call by name this wayward son who returned home with the intention of asking to be accepted, not as a son or heir, but as one of his father's hired servants?

However, that wayward son receives much more commendation than he actually deserves, for if he had been granted what he had intended to ask of his father, he would have been numbered among those hired servants who were now being dispatched to make preparations for his welcome back home.

According to some of the earlier New Testament manuscripts, the son was not even allowed to finish his contemplated plea that he be permitted to return as one of those servants (v. 21).

Has not this prodigal son, illustrating the loving, gracious attitude of God and his own Son Jesus, too long and too emphatically been permitted to overshadow the One who is actually the central, important figure in this fascinating story—God, the compassionate Father himself?

It would therefore be even more wonderful to be able to identify, at least by name, this compassionate father who exemplifies the graciousness of our heavenly Father who sent his own Son into this world not to become a prodigal nor simply to welcome prodigal humans back to God but to provide the way and the means of our being permitted and able to go home to be with God, not as servants, but as joint heirs with his own Son, Christ Jesus?

This interpretation is not only in complete accord with Jesus' objective in relating this fascinating story but also parallels the details of the story. What, for instance, did this wayward son have to commend himself? Had he not voluntarily left home with his share of the inheritance? Had he not squandered it wantonly, living it up till he had nothing left? Had he not gone, not to the dogs, but to the hogs—which to those Israelites was the very depth of degradation—being compelled to eat hog food because no one would offer him anything better? Did he not recognize his own depraved condition when he decided to beg his own father to receive him, not as his son, but merely as one of his hired servants?

It is also in complete harmony with Jesus' declared purpose in descending into this world, not to be served but to serve, and to give his life as a ransom for many (see Matt. 20:28).

When Jesus told Matthew to follow him, Matthew honored him with a banquet, to which he also invited a number of tax collectors and other friends. The Pharisees raised the same question which prompted Jesus to relate this incident. On that occasion Jesus responded: "They who are in good health have no need of a physician, but those who are ill do. I did not come to call righteous people, but sinners" (Luke 5:31).

This is substantiated also as we read on in this well-known parable to a portion which, unfortunately, is *not* so well-known—the bitter, hostile reaction of that elder son who, when he came to the house and learned the reason for that celebration, became bitterly resentful. Because of the father's royal reception of that prodigal brother of his, he refused to go inside.

This is actually the climax of the entire story. The scribes and Pharisees were vigorously objecting to Jesus' mingling with those who needed him most, to his extending God's compassion to *all* of us sinful mortals, based not upon our worthiness but upon our need, our condition.

75

As it was questioned during Jesus' life on earth, this objective is still misunderstood and criticized by many today, causing costly negligence on the part of his professed followers.

Therefore the title traditionally given to this story (which, incidentally, is not recorded in the biblical account itself), is a misleading misnomer. The emphasis should be placed upon *The Compassionate Father*.

On Second Thought

Matthew 21:28-32

It would be easy to pass over lightly this illustration. One of the sons answers his father: "Yes, I'll go," but doesn't. The other son says: "No, I'm *not* going," but later changes his mind and goes. So what? Wasn't the work done?

Or *was* the work done, in the manner in which the father had planned? And who did the portion which that other son *failed* to do?

The chief priests and elders demanded to know on what authority Jesus had cleaned out the Temple—for the second time (see John 2:13 ff.).

"I'll answer your question," the Master responded, "if you will answer mine. The baptism of John, whence was it, of heaven or of men?"

After a discussion among themselves, they gave this evasive response: "We don't know."

"Neither am I telling you," Jesus told them, "with what authority I am doing this" (vv. 24-27).

Was Jesus deliberately evading their question? On the contrary, he was implying much more than those Temple authorities were willing to concede. Many of the Israelites, including a number from there in Jerusalem, had gone out into the wilderness to hear John's message and to be baptized. However, when John pointed to him and called him the Lamb of God, many of them did not follow Jesus.

Now their leaders were once more rejecting Jesus, unwilling to acknowledge that the Temple was, as Jesus had declared to them, "My Father's house" (see v. 13).

What effect did the decisions and redecisions of these two sons have upon their subsequent attitudes and conduct with reference to their father? This is actually of far less significance than the application which Jesus now makes.

Although many of those Israelites who had heard John turned away, many others were now turning and following Jesus. He tells them that soon they would see many of the tax collectors and those whom they classified as sinners entering the kingdom of God while they themselves would remain on the outside because they were rejecting him whom God had promised and had now sent into the world. Jesus was to be rejected and crucified at the request of those to whom God had given the wonderful opportunity of sharing him with the rest of mankind.

As history has verified, Jesus was actually foretelling to these Temple authorities the tragic truth that they would actually be changing places with those Gentile sinners whom they were looking down upon with disdain. They who professed to be working for God were now actually changing their minds, having second thoughts, and not doing God's will, while those hated, despised sinners out there who had not known God would also change their minds and begin following and serving God.

Second thoughts have much greater weight than we may realize. In many instances they actually determine or alter the entire course of one's life and are therefore of far greater importance or weight than those first thoughts, which frequently come on the spur of the moment or may be the result of previous thinking or habits, which are not easily altered or broken.

With reference to their reactions or manner of thinking, individuals may be classified in either of three groups. There are those who pause to think before they act or react. There are others who do their thinking while they are acting or reacting—but in time to avert, or at least alleviate, undesirable or catastrophic results. And there are those who carry out their original decisions or intentions and do their thinking afterward, when it is too late, regretting—if indeed they live to regret—their original hasty decisions or actions.

It is so easy to give a ready answer, to exercise snap judgment.

Quite frequently this is done with a burst of enthusiasm which quickly cools off, as in the case of this first son: "Yes, of course I'll go out and work today." It is often done merely to "save face." Then: "But after thinking it over . . . ."

Such expressions as these are also frequently heard: "Oh, but I didn't mean that." "I didn't realize what I was saying." "Did I say that? I don't remember." "Oh, I didn't mean to say that!" "Oh, forget that!"

This brings to mind those words of warning which Jesus spoke to those who will say in the judgment: "Lord, Lord, did we not in your name prophesy, and in your name cast out demons, and in your name do many powerful things?" "And then," the Lord continues, "I shall acknowledge to them: 'I never knew you; depart from me, workers of iniquity'" (Matt. 7:22 f.).

How much better are those second thoughts such as that of this second son, thoughts that are acted upon before it is too late. A change of mind or of intention of this nature can be made without embarrassment or regret.

Why Shouldn't He?

Matthew 21:33-46

When the Sadducees questioned Jesus' authority for cleansing the Temple, he related to them the story of a landlord who rented his vineyard to laborers who not only mistreated and killed his servants whom he sent for his share of the crop but also killed his own son whom he sent, intending to take over his inheritance.

However, instead of making the application, he put the question to them: "Therefore, when the owner of the vineyard returns, what is he going to do to those laborers?" (v. 40).

The effectiveness of the Master's illustration is revealed by the Sadducees' response; this common Greek assonance is actually quite difficult to translate adequately into English. "He will put the wretches to a wretched death," according to one translation, [1] "and will rent out the vineyard to other farm-laborers who will give him the fruits in their season" (v. 41).

78

What further proof could those hostile religious leaders have needed of Jesus' authority to clean up his Father's house? What could they expect God to do to *them* if they continued to reject and dishonor his own Son, finally delivering him to the Roman authorities, demanding that he be crucified?

The ironic aftermath of this confrontation in the Temple was that those self-righteous Sadducees, after passing sentence upon those rebellious laborers in that vineyard, were so infuriated because of the teaching and ministry of the Son of the Owner of the Vineyard in which they were laboring that they went out and plotted with their fellow laborers to have *him* killed.

What stronger proof of Jesus' authority could one want than that which Jesus is conveying with this powerful illustration? What else could God be expected to do under such circumstances after humans living in his vineyard deliberately reject his only begotten Son thus consenting to his death? As the author of the book of Hebrews so forcefully puts it, they are recrucifying for themselves the Son of God and putting him to open shame (Heb. 6:6).

Quite frequently such comments as these are heard: "I wouldn't want a God who would send a person to hell," or "God is too good to send anyone to hell."

As a matter of fact God *is* too good to send anyone to hell. That is why he sent his only begotten Son into this world, to live, to die, and to conquer death by rising and returning to heaven to make intercession to his heavenly Father. Jesus went to prepare a place for those of us humans who will not reject him and who will put our trust in him.

The landlord of this vineyard has a clear and vitally important message for the multitudes living today who are guilty of conduct meriting the same treatment awaiting these rebellious, conniving laborers. The multitudes of today are living in and enjoying God's world but are not willing to submit to his will by yielding their lives and their efforts to his Son. And Jesus did not come to this earth merely to receive God's share of the fruits of their labor but to also invite them to enjoy the fruits of *his* labor, not only in this life but in the great beyond, with him.

What is more, those belligerent Temple authorities have also, and unwittingly, left posterity a very important and imperative lesson—

79

that it is much simpler to pass judgment upon someone else and to describe the deserved punishment than to acknowledge one's own guilt and admit that this same punishment should be administered to them, as well as to others. Does this not make their own punishment even more deserved?

[1] Compare the Weymouth translation here.

Justified Sinner

Luke 18:9-14

"And he also spoke this parable to some of those who had in themselves the confidence that they were righteous and despised everyone else" (v. 9).

Inasmuch, then, as there were at that time so many to whom the illustration would apply, we would certainly be justified in inferring that these two men to whom Jesus referred were living beings and not merely illustrative characters. It is even possible that during one of his visits to the Temple Jesus had actually observed the two.

Opening with this narrative statement, "Two men went up into the temple to pray," Jesus continues: "The Pharisee prayed these things to himself: 'God, I thank you that I am not just like the rest of the men, . . . or even like this tax-collector.' "

Then he proceeds to enumerate some of the things that he *does;* he fasts twice a week—more often than the Law required, and gives a tenth of what he receives, both according to pharisaical tradition.

When he compared himself with that despised tax collector, he doubtless looked behind him to where that individual was standing at a distance, not even presuming to lift up his eyes while beating his breast, the traditional gesture of contrition, as he breathed his simple, humble petition: "God, have mercy on me, the sinner."

This man actually had more against him than his failure or refusal to pattern his life after the pharisaical traditions. His position as a tax collector for a foreign government, carrying with it the privilege of retaining for himself whatever he succeeded in collecting above the taxes required by the Roman authorities, made the members of his profession unpopular, not only with the Pharisees but with other Israelites as well.

Was this man measuring himself according to the standards of that Pharisee standing up there in front of him and commending himself before God? Or was he admitting his shortcomings according to the standards of *God?*

As a matter of fact, he was not seeking to commend himself in the sight of God but, as an admitted sinner, was imploring God for undeserved mercy.

This suggests a vitally important question: By whose standards are we human beings evaluated? The predominance of public opinion is that individuals are evaluated and justified by their own philosophies or standards, according to their own opinions and their own thinking—or lack of thinking.

This brings to mind the dismal note on which the book of the judges of Israel is concluded: "In those days . . . every man did what was right in his own eyes" (Judg. 21:25).

And so this penitent sinner has a message out of the past for the people of our enlightened and sophisticated era, a message, in fact, direly needed by multitudes who are relying upon their own self-righteousness to commend them to God—and many of them do not even recognize the existence of God.

This repentant sinner's humble, profound prayer has become a model petition for many who, like him, seek God's unmerited mercy and grace. And they too have the assurance that when this prayer is uttered in humble sincerity, as in the case of this tax collector, God will recognize and answer.

Poor Rich Man

Luke 16:19-31   And a certain man was rich.

As Jesus introduces this in narrative form, it would be logical to conclude that he is speaking of someone who had actually lived, died, and experienced the torment described.

The man's postmortem experience and conversation with "Father

Abraham" are deserving of much more consideration than has been given to them.

Every day the wealthy man dressed in the height of fashion and lived luxuriously. And every day an incapacitated begger named Lazarus was carried to the rich man's gate, hoping to be fed with scraps that fell from the rich man's table. Whether he actually received any of those scraps we are not informed; in fact, the language seems to indicate that he did not.

Even the dogs that came looking for some of those scraps were more friendly; instead of growling or snapping at him, they licked the poor man's sores.

When the rich man died, he was buried. When the poor man died, "he was carried away to the bosom of Abraham" (v. 22). Does this not emphasize the relative unimportance of the human body after death when the immortal soul is taken from it?

We are also reminded that the possession and enjoyment of material possessions here on earth are not as meaningful as what we do or fail to do under the circumstances in which we may find ourselves—as well as what we do or fail to do for others—particularly those who are less fortunate than ourselves.

Jesus is emphasizing also the finality of death, the absolute impossibility for those failing to make provision in this life for the life to come to pass through that great gulf separating that individual from eternal life with God.

Notice further that even now the wealthy man does not address himself to God, but makes his pathetic appeal to "Father Abraham." Could this not be due to his having depended in this life upon human knowledge and tradition, instead of endeavoring to know and seek the will of God? Many to whom Jesus spoke during his earthly ministry did that. Many are doing so today.

The man's utter depravity under those terrible circumstances is revealed by his pathetic plea—a mere drop of cold water on the tip of Lazarus' finger for relief from that tortuous flame. He reveals no semblance of regret or repentance—only the desire for that ridiculously infinitesimal temporary relief (v. 24)—and notice, at the hand of the man who here on earth had daily been at his mercy! One wonders whether he had actually spanned that gulf which separated them at that time.

Now he is pleading with Abraham to send Lazarus back to warn his five brothers to avoid that terrible place of eternal torment.

The response to this plea is of tremendous significance: "They have Moses and the prophets; let them listen to them." Still the man insists, and still the response is: "If they don't listen to them, neither will they be persuaded if someone rises from the dead" (vv. 30 f.).

One of Lazarus' greatest difficulties would have been that of convincing those five brothers that he had actually returned from the realm of the dead.

And now in addition to what that man's brothers had, we have the New Testament containing other reminders and warnings from the Lord Jesus himself; all of this is amply sufficient and is the only means of avoiding that place of terrible torment.

Unfortunate indeed is it that too scant attention has been focused upon the man's tragic situation and pathetic plea. The undeniable unpleasantness of his eternal suffering should never be permitted to overshadow this significant warning which the Savior has so graciously left for posterity. Surely that poor rich man would not want this message to be soft-pedaled.

Nor would the Master have thus drawn aside that veil separating us from the realm of the departed dead to warn us—on the strength of the man's plea—that this message be dispatched to earth to warn those who direly need that warning. And who does *not* need this timey warning?

His urgent plea will in fact lose none of its vital significance as long as human beings remain upon this earth. And yet how many— or should we say how *few*—are heeding his clarion warning?

Although we know the name of the poor beggar, we do not actually know the name of that poor rich man. *Dives,* the name traditionally ascribed to him, is the Latin word for "rich, wealthy," which introduces the incident in the Latin Vulgate translation of the Bible. The word in the original Greek text is *plousios.* His name could just as well be Plousios—or perhaps even Rich!

As a matter of fact, well might it be Legion, for unfortunately and tragically he represents a great multitude of every era. This multitude enjoy God's material universe here on earth while without giving any heed to their eternal destiny. Nor do they take thought of the Supreme Being who created and sustains them and who is able and willing to redeem them and share with them something much better, more glamorous, and longer enduring than earth— that place where the rich man's contemporary, Lazarus, is now.

Builders

Matthew 7:24-29

Whether or not these two men, of whom the Lord Jesus speaks in concluding his great masterpiece known as the Sermon on the Mount, were living persons, they represent two large groups of individuals—as a matter of fact, the entire human race as indicated by the manner in which he presents them: "Everyone who hears these my words and does them . . ." (v. 24), "and everyone hearing these my words and not doing them . . ." (v. 26).

The Lord does not describe the structures which these two men built; the comparison which he makes has to do with the *foundations* upon which they built—the one upon rock, the other upon sand.

The real test of a structure lies not in what either the architect or the builder might have had in mind but in the durability of the finished structure itself. The test came not when these two houses were completed but when they were exposed to the elements. When the rain, wind, and floods came, the house built upon the rock foundation withstood their force. That house built upon the sand was demolished—regardless of the manner in which it had been constructed.

This, says Jesus, is a portrayal of the manner in which individuals plan and live their lives, depicting also the outcome of their lives.

The scribes and Pharisees passed along the traditional interpretations handed down to them, interpretations of what the Law of God was supposed to mean.

Here stood One who was not voicing mere traditional opinions or interpretations. He spoke with the wisdom and the authority of the Eternal God himself, whom he not only represented but of whom he was also the Incarnation. He was therefore in a position to declare:

"You have heard that it was said . . . But *I* tell you . . ." (Matt. 5:21 ff.).

In the light of everything which Jesus, the Son of God, has presented, the imperative importance of this closing illustration of these two men who built their houses cannot be overestimated. He deals not with abstract theories or speculations, embellished with fancy oratory, but with truth and consequences. He deals with two life patterns which are different in both their objectives and their ultimate destinations and which involve our relationships not only with our fellowmen but also with our Creator, Sustainer, and Redeemer—yes, and our Judge.

Many of us are now passing judgment upon God, and upon Jesus his Son. The time is coming, however, when God, not they, will be sitting in judgment, and *his* judgment will be final.

These two buildings were not put to the test, it should be remembered, until the rain, flood, and wind came upon them. Suppose, however, that the man who built upon the sand foundation had been made aware of his error before the elements descended; what could he have done to prevent that catastrophe? He might have reasoned that since his structure built on the sand foundation looked as strong as that built upon the rock foundation, it would surely withstand bad weather. Or he could have decided to run the risk, "take a chance." Otherwise it would have been necessary to move it to a firmer foundation or abandon it altogether; in either case, extra effort and expense would have been necessary.

On the other hand, when that storm came, was not the house a total loss? Is this not typical of human lives which are being built upon insecure foundations?

When it became necessary to enlarge the surgical department of a hospital, the decision was made to add several stories to that wing of the building. However, they were informed that the foundation was not strong enough to support those additional floors. The entire wing was torn down, the foundation reenforced, and an entirely new structure erected. Was not this a tremendous waste of time, money, and labor?

But suppose they had taken the risk of building on that old structure and the entire building had collapsed? The conclusion is obvious.

This is the situation which an individual confronts, before it is too late, when he learns that he has been building his entire life structure on an insecure foundation, and under the direction of the

Holy Spirit a new life structure is started and is grounded upon the Rock, Christ Jesus, a structure so firmly grounded that there is no power that can destroy it.

But, oh! when that final test comes and one discovers, too late, that the foundation on which he has been building his life structure cannot withstand the final test and crumbles! Then shall that one hear those fateful words spoken by the Savior immediately before giving this illustration: "I never knew you; depart from me, workers of iniquity (lawlessness)" (Matt. 7:23).

How gracious the Lord Jesus has been to show us humans how to build and not only to tell us upon what foundation to build but to become that Foundation!

Not Following Us

Mark 9:38-40; Luke 9:49-50

After Jesus had rebuked his disciples for holding a popularity contest to determine which of them was the greatest, John, perhaps to "save face," told him that when they saw a man casting out evil spirits in his name, they told him to stop doing that.

It was not the nature of the deed itself to which they objected. As a matter of fact, he was doing something which Jesus himself was doing and had sent them out to do.

From the nature of John's complaint we can safely infer that the man was not only trying to heal those demoniacs, but was actually succeeding; had he failed, John would certainly have said so.

For what reason, then, had they ordered the man to stop? "Because he was not following with us" (Mark 9:38).

Were *they* not his chosen disciples? Had *they* not been following him all this time? Had he not sent *them* out to heal and to cast out evil spirits? What right had that outsider to be doing what *they* were sent out to do?

John, the "son of thunder," might possibly be commended for his loyalty to his Master. Nevertheless, this is overshadowed by several other things that should be taken into consideration.

This outsider's ability or success in casting out evil spirits should have caused John and the other disciples to engage in serious introspection, self-examination.

A short time previous to this, the disciples who had remained at the foot of the mount of transfiguration had failed in their effort to cast an evil spirit out of a boy whose father had brought him to Jesus to be healed (Matt. 17:14-20).

When they asked why it was that they had been unable to heal the boy, he told them their failure was due to their not having prayed and not relying on *his* power to do the healing. Had he not instructed them previously to go out and minister *in his name?*

Why could they not realize that this stranger was doing what those disciples were unable to do because he was relying upon the power of Jesus and not upon his own ability to do the healing?

Could it be possible also that John and his brother James were too deeply concerned about sitting on either side of Jesus' throne in glory [1] to be concerned about having a part in the great work of him whose Father sent him into this world, not to be ministered unto but to serve and to lay down his own life that others might have the opportunity of living in heaven with him?

And perhaps it had not occurred to them that with his divine power Jesus himself had moved that man to perform that act of mercy which John himself did not perform—and endeavored to prevent the outsider from performing.

There are those who, like these disciples, seem to have the impression that it is better for good deeds not to be performed at all unless performed by "the right people." Who, after all, determines who those right people are? Good does not become evil merely because it is not done by those who consider themselves especially chosen to do that particular type of work.

And who knows how much good is left undone because those "right people" fail to take advantage of their opportunities?

Jesus also made this significant statement on this occasion: "For he who is not against us is for us" (Luke 9:50).

Sorcerers would endeavor to perform miracles in the name of Jesus but for their own glory and benefit—with disastrous consequences (Acts 19:13-16).

On the other hand, others besides the eleven disciples would be chosen and empowered to perform miracles and render other services in Jesus' name.

Years later, when that ardent persecutor of Christians went to Damascus to bring back those who had fled from Jerusalem, the Lord Jesus stopped, regenerated, and commissioned him to spread the message of salvation to the Gentiles. Saul of Tarsus was certainly the last man whom the disciples would have dared to approach with the good news—and certainly with an assignment such as the Lord gave to him!

But Saul of Tarsus actually accomplished much more than *all* of those disciples together. However, in writing of his experiences, Paul not only expresses his unworthiness to be called an apostle but adds humbly and reverently, "yet not I, but the grace of God which was with me" (1 Cor. 15:10).

And certainly Saul of Tarsus was the last man whom those disciples would have dared to approach with the gospel—or with an assignment such as Jesus gave him, to proclaim the good news to the Gentiles.

And had you noticed? When that zealous Pharisee made it so dangerous for the followers of Jesus to remain in Jerusalem that they were scattered to Judea and Samaria, those who did not leave the city were the apostles; those who did leave began spreading the gospel (Acts 8:1 ff.).

[1] Matthew 20:20-23; Mark 9:33-34.

Shrewd Steward

Luke 16:1-13

And now we have the case of a household steward or financial manager of an estate who not only placed himself and his employer in difficult situations but has also left biblical scholars a perplexing problem.

When his employer was informed that he had been mismanaging the estate, calling the steward in, he notified him that his services were no longer required.

Now what was the man going to do? He was not a skilled or trained laborer, and he would be ashamed to beg.

He decided to solve the problem by calling in his employer's debtors and reducing the size of their debts, so that later, when he needed help and approached them, they would feel obligated to do something for him.

The problem left for us is to learn why Jesus encouraged his followers to profit by the example of a man with such a questionable reputation. Surely the Son of God would not suggest that we befriend children of mammon by doing things which they do and thus becoming like them?

And how, we might ask, could people like this conniving steward and his associates become eligible for admission into God's eternal abodes?

Neither this steward nor his employer profited immediately by the deal with those debtors. As a matter of fact the latter lost even more. Then what reason did he have for commending the man for being so shrewd? He did so because of the man's foresightedness in thus paving the way for his own future.

Although Jesus declares that the children of this world are actually wiser than the children of God, he does not suggest that we become as shrewd as they are. What he does urge is that we be even *more shrewd* than this man proved to be.

That the Lord is using this man as a *negative* example of what we Christians should do is substantiated by what he says immediately following: "No servant is able to serve two masters; for he will either hate the one and love the other, or he will hold on to the one, and despise the other; you are unable to serve God and mammon (possessions, wealth)" (Luke 16:13; see also Matt. 6:24).

By means of the illustration of the clever but unscrupulous steward, Jesus presents to us a vital threefold challenge.

First of all, although we no longer desire to do things which the people of the world do, he is urging us not to isolate ourselves completely from them and not to be influenced by them but to place ourselves in a position *to influence them.* Herein lies one of the difficult problems confronting sincere Christians and yet one of the most challenging opportunities.

This is clearly indicated by the reason which the Lord gives, that when *our* turn comes to enter those eternal abodes of glory, *they* may be there, waiting to extend us a hearty welcome because we will have been instrumental in their being able to enter those eternal abodes.

If, on the other hand, we continue living the same life which they are living, doing the same things which they are doing, we are going to leave with them the impression that there is actually no difference between them and us; therefore, why should *they* become followers of our Savior and Lord?

One is likely to hear something like this: "If so-and-so is a member of your church, then I don't want to be." They know too much about those individuals. And the only thing that *we* can do is to set a better example for them.

If in cultivating their friendship we constantly, but wisely and tactfully let them discern that, because of our relationship with our Savior, our life pattern has been transformed, we will be in a better position to influence them to turn to him.

In the second place, to put this same thought negatively, if we lose their respect by failing to show them the positive side of the Christlike life, we actually become indebted to them by keeping them from entering that eternal realm of glory.

In the third place, capitalize on your friendship with them—and herein lies the crux of this illustration—by making them eternally grateful and indebted to you for making it possible for them to be able to welcome you into glory.

Therefore, rather than leaving us, through his negative example, a difficult or perplexing problem, this steward of questionable character actually presents us with a vitally important challenge to capitalize, as Jesus points out, on his negative example. Thus we would act more wisely, more profitably than do the children of mammon, of the world, hence making people indebted to us not in terms of the coin of the realm but of eternal glory.

Remuneration

Matthew 19:27 to 20:16

"What do I get out of this?" "What's in it for me?"

This in substance is what Simon Peter asked the Lord Jesus—questions we hear frequently in our own era.

Although the parable with which Jesus augmented his response would cause laborers and their leaders to revolt and walk out in disgust, careful examination reveals the depth of Jesus' logic and spiritual significance.

A landlord goes out to the marketplace one morning to find laborers to work in his vineyard. He goes out several times during the day, even as late as the eleventh hour.

At the close of the workday, he gives each of them a denarius, undoubtedly a fair wage in those days, beginning with those whom he had employed at the last hour.

Those who had toiled all day waited expectantly. When they received no more than those who had worked one hour, they were astounded, furious. What sort of business was this, anyway?

At least one of them either refused to pick up his wage or, as has been suggested, might possibly have thrown it down in anger, in view of what the employer said to him. He actually answered him courteously: "Friend, pick up your money and get out."

After all, he inquired, was he not paying them what he had agreed? What is more, had he not gone out there and found *all* of them standing idle in the marketplace?

The significance of this incident is forcefully brought out by what the Savior then repeats to the disciples, what is going to take place after their arrival in Jerusalem, the sacrifice of his own life as the price for their eternal salvation—and, we might add, our salvation also.

To carry out the thought in this parable, he was giving them the opportunity of being among those serving in his vineyard, instead of their being among those waiting outside for whatever might await them out there.

Many of us, like Simon Peter, are inclined to think in terms of what we have given up after becoming Christians, also of what we are now doing, either for our Savior, for our church, or perhaps for others and of what we hope or expect to receive as reward in the hereafter.

Perhaps we are thinking in terms of another of Jesus' parables, of a landlord who, before going away, gave a sum of money to each of his servants according to their ability. Upon returning, he gave each the money which he had earned, giving the money which one of them had earned to him who had earned the greatest amount.

At first glance these two parables may seem to be in direct conflict or contradiction. The contrast is brought out by what this landlord says to those disgruntled day laborers:

"Was this not my money? And couldn't I do what I wanted with it? And haven't I given to each of you what I had promised? one denarius?"

Now try to imagine what heaven would be like if, on that wonderful foundation which the Redeemer has laid at so tremendous a price, instead of rejecting us, as he will reject those who reject him and his wonderful provision for their salvation, all of us who are redeemed would be permitted to build our own superstructure, displaying what *we* have done for *him*—or would it *actually be for him?* (1 Cor. 3:10-15).

How would heaven differ from what we have here on earth, with each of us strutting about singing our own praises, wearing our own crowns instead of laying them at his feet and bowing to him in worshipful adoration because of all that he has done for us?

The real test is not what we expect to receive from him because of what we may have given up to follow him, but what *we owe him* because of *what he has done for us*—without which we would not even be accorded the privilege of seeing the kingdom of heaven.

Where, then, do works enter into the picture? Should we sit down and fold our hands and sing his praises? Herein lies the significance of this landlord's message to us: As those day laborers, instead of being idle all day, were privileged to work in that vineyard, we who are privileged to enter the kingdom of God should gladly do all in our power to demonstrate our gratitude.

It would be more appropriate for our Savior to ask, "After all that I have done for you, what am *I* going to get out of it?"

Mighty Mites

Mark 12:41-44; Luke 21:1-4

Many of those who were bringing their gifts to the Temple were casting their brass and copper coins into the treasury with sufficient clang to call others' attention to the fact that they were making their offering.

How much attention was attracted by two coins of the smallest denomination currently in circulation—smaller than our proverbial "thin dime," yes, even much smaller than our copper penny—contributed by this poor widow?

After casting in the coins, she quickly vanished in the crowd.

However, special attention was given to her by one who was sitting nearby, observing. He did not embarrass the poor woman by what he said or by pointing her out to the crowd. But calling his disciples to his side, he informed them:

"I tell you truly that this poor widow has put into the treasury more than all of those casting into it" (Mark 12:43).

Was Jesus inferring that the woman had contributed more than any one of them or all of them together? In the light of what he said further, either interpretation is possible. Certainly a strong case can be made for the latter interpretation.

"The widow's mite" has been adopted as the standard of giving by many who claim credit equal to that which has been given to this poor widow. However, they have misinterpreted this on two counts.

In the first place, she has been given only *half* as much credit she rightfully merits. She gave, not *one,* but *two* mites, or *lepta,* thin copper coins, each of which would be equivalent to no more than one fifth of one of our copper pennies.

In the second place, they fail to recognize that which Jesus actually pointed out to the disciples. They measure their giving in terms of *the size of her gift,* whereas Jesus did not *mention* the size of the gift; he commended her not for the gift itself but in terms of *what she had left.*

"For they," he said, "cast in out of their abundance (their superfluity), but she out of her poverty put in all that she had, *her entire livelihood.*

Note also now that Jesus did not rebuke or even criticize the others who were throwing in their offerings. As he declared on another occasion, he had not come into this world to judge (or condemn) the world, but rather that the world through him might be saved (John 3:17).

They had the law of Moses, and they also had the example of their forefather Abraham (Gen. 14:17-20), both of which those Israelites should have been familiar.

And something which Jesus said on another occasion would also apply here, something which many of us Christians too frequently overlook or fail to apply to ourselves: "They have their reward" (see also Matt. 6:2,3,16).

If this unnamed widow were to speak to us today, what would be her message, especially to those who have been giving her half as much credit as she deserves and overlooking altogether the vital point which the Master made to the disciples, her proportionate giving—"her entire livelihood"?

Or, because of her modesty and perhaps her embarrassment due to her inability to give an amount comparable with the gifts of other contributors, would she, as on this occasion, slip away unnoticed in the crowd?

Persistence Provocative

Luke 18:1-8   Lest persistently coming she wear me out.

Inasmuch as Luke quotes the Lord Jesus as saying, "There was a certain judge . . ." then adds, "A certain widow was in that city . . ." there should be little doubt that he is relating an event that actually occurred.

Who would expect a hardhearted, "hard-boiled" judge, who neither feared God nor had any regard for men, to continue to be pestered by a poor widow simply because someone was making life miserable for *her?* What could this poor woman expect or even vaguely hope to receive from a prominent person of his temperament?

As a matter of fact, he might even be annoyed to the point of defending her adversary in order to be rid of the pestiferous woman!

Nevertheless, his continued indifference notwithstanding, she implored him time after time to take her case.

"Now listen," Jesus continues, "to what this judge finally decides: "Even though I do not fear God nor have any respect for man, yet because this widow is annoying me so, I'm going to defend her, lest coming repeatedly (to the very end) she wear me out." This was his only reason for changing his mind and yielding to her repeated requests.

And now notice the challenging application which the Lord makes of this illustration: "Listen to what this unrighteous (unscrupulous) judge is saying. And so will God not bring about the vindication of his chosen ones who are crying to him day and night, and be patient (long-suffering) toward them?"

And he adds these words of reassurance: "I tell you that he will bring about their vindication quickly."

However, Jesus does not stop here. He enhances this challenge even further by asking: "Nevertheless, when the Son of man comes, is he really going to find faith upon the earth?" (v. 8).

It is also well to remind ourselves in this connection of that statement which Jesus made when speaking of that unjust steward: "The sons of men are wiser in their generation than the sons of God" (Luke 16:8). What an indictment! And yet how tragically true!

Unfortunate indeed is it that so many of God's children, "joint heirs with his Son, Jesus," with all of the spiritual resources which God through him has placed at our disposition, so frequently fail to exercise the persistence displayed by this importunate widow.

She kept "bugging" that arrogant judge, with little assurance of the desired results but because she desperately needed his assistance.

God, on the other hand, *urges* us to come to him with our needs, our desires, our problems, our petitions, not with arrogance but with boldness—not because *we* think it should be that way but because God's only begotten Son has made this possible.

What was Jesus' motive in relating this story of that hard-hearted judge and this persistent widow?

"To the end that it is necessary for them always to pray, and not to grow weary (to lose heart)" (v. 1).

Therefore what reason, what excuse has the earnest, sincere Christian for failing or refusing to reach out in *bold*, reverent faith to his or her loving, gracious heavenly Father, imploring him in the name of his Son who extended this invitation to supply our needs and to grant our sincere desires?

"Oh, what's the use? Why bother God with this?" "How do I know he'll give me what I want?" "I prayed about something once, but it did no good." "I don't know how to pray." These are among the numerous excuses which are frequently heard.

We should keep in mind several things of which James in his epistle points out to us (Jas. 4:1-4), that, although we have not because we do not ask, yet on the other hand we ask and do not receive because we ask for selfish reasons, for our own lusts.

What a message Jesus has sent by means of this troubled but persistent widow to those of us who, by our example if not admittedly, classify ourselves with those of little faith!

How Many Times?

Matthew 18:21-35

Peter undoubtedly expected the Master to commend him for asking such a question as this. Seven times should surely be sufficient— yes, *more* than enough.

What must his reaction have been when Jesus responded: "I don't tell you as often as *seven* times, but as much as *seventy times* seven" (v. 22).

And what a marvelous illustration which the Savior has related to reenforce his amazing answer!

When this first servant who was called in for a reckoning pleads for mercy because of his inability to pay his debt, the king not only liberates him from the severe punishment which he would have suffered, but also cancels his entire debt.

Is it any wonder that when his fellow servants hear how he treats another servant they report it to the king, who then revokes his pardon and compels him to pay his debt?

The full significance of this incident is revealed by a comparison of the amount which this first servant owes the *king* with that which his fellow servant owes *him.*

The value of a talent was 6,000 denarii. This first servant's debt of 10,000 talents was therefore 600,000 times the 100 denarii owed him by that fellow servant—*sixty million denarii!*

In the light of these comparative figures, can Jesus' answer be considered a gross, hypothetical exaggeration? Not when considered in the light of the tremendous debt of sin which the Savior wiped out for Peter.

To what extent can anyone be indebted to those of us who have been redeemed by Jesus? At so tremendous a price through the shedding of his blood on Calvary, do we hold anyone accountable for anything which may have been done to provoke, to offend, or to injure us in the light of the great debt of sin which Jesus has wiped out for us so that we might, through him, inherit eternal life?

How often we Christians become angry, resentful, cold, and indifferent and even break off relations with someone whom we are reluctant or unwilling to forgive for something done to us—even for something which we may *imagine* to have been done?

We may find it difficult, perhaps impossible, to forgive someone for something which we may consider a major offense. Nevertheless, it can be done by exercising a sufficient amount of effort and willpower with God's help, always keeping in mind the sacrifice which Jesus willingly made to clear our debt of sin, which is far greater than anything which an offending individual could possibly do to harm or irritate us.

It should be remembered also that God does not wait for us to approach him and ask for his forgiveness. Through his Holy Spirit and through the instrumentality of someone who has already been forgiven and has approached us with the good news of God's offer of forgiveness, not for merely one transgression, but for *all* of them, no matter what or how great they may be, the price has been paid.

Suppose someone does not ask for forgiveness, does not even admit the offense (which you know has been committed). Or suppose someone asks to be forgiven then offends you again, perhaps many times and in that same manner.

The Lord Jesus gives us the answer at the close of this incident— *"from your hearts"* (v. 35). This will of course benefit *you* more than it will the guilty party. And should you grow weary of such treatment, think of the many times God has forgiven you when you have repeatedly sinned against *him.*

And should this be repeated too many times, it is your prerogative to avoid further dealings with that individual.

There is that ugly monster, Revenge, "getting even with" someone who has offended us, or who we *think* has offended us. But this makes matters worse, widening the breach and often paving the way for further ill will and difficulty.

The cause and kingdom of our Lord Jesus Christ has been greatly hindered because of the manner in which Christians react toward fellow Christians, also toward others who could have been attracted to our Savior if we had revealed toward them the same attitude as that which the Lord has manifested toward us!

What a message this unforgiving servant has left for our era, which differs little from that in which he lived! How many times do we find ourselves in a situation similar to his? And how many times are we inclined to ask this same question which Simon Peter asked of the Savior?

Home Missionary

Mark 5:1-20

Is it difficult to understand why a man who had lived among the dead, unclothed, raving mad, mutilating himself, too powerful to be chained, feared by everyone would desire to go away with the one who had restored him to sanity? This one restored him so that he could now wear clothes without ripping them off and could sit down calmly. This man was now an object of amazement rather than one of fear and dread apprehension.

In addition to deep gratitude and devotion, he would have other reasons for desiring to follow his Benefactor. Those familiar surroundings could have lingering memories of that dread past. And what about the comments which his neighbors were likely to make from time to time? People are very thoughtless and inconsiderate under such circumstances.

There was a still stronger reason for his desiring to leave—the reaction of the owners of those hogs. Was he not the cause of their losing them? And were they not insisting that his Healer leave the country? They might take vengeance on him, even insist that he also leave or perhaps drive him out to the tombs again, even place him in chains to prevent a possible relapse—instead of rejoicing over his miraculous restoration to sanity. People react strangely under such circumstances, particularly when their personal economic welfare is involved.

Then why did Jesus instruct him to remain at home?

He wanted him to show and tell his family, his neighbors, his friends what Jesus had done for him.

But had Jesus not admonished others whom he had healed to tell *no one*—for example, that leper who, despite Jesus' admonition, went everywhere telling everyone, making it necessary for Jesus to avoid the cities because of the multitudes bringing their impotent to be healed? (Mark 1:40-45).

This was a different situation. People in Capernaum and throughout Galilee had seen what Jesus was doing and were bringing their afflicted to be healed, but they were not responding to his good news of salvation through repentance and faith in him. He was therefore going elsewhere, including this region of the Gerasenes, where not even his miraculous healing was making an impression.

Who would be in a better position to remind them of their materialistic mania (putting greater value on hogs) which could be replaced, than upon the welfare of their kinsman and neighbor with whose tragic condition they had been unable to cope?

Suppose Jesus had permitted this man to accompany him. Not only would he have missed the opportunity to witness there at home, where his testimony was so greatly needed; he might have been swallowed up in that throng following Jesus from place to place, curious to see more of the miracles which Jesus would perform or seeking to minister to him who had come not to be ministered to but to minister (Mark 10:45).

How effective in his own country was the witness of this living example of what the Son of God could do for needy humanity?

Later when Jesus landed not far away on the shore of Gadara, recognizing who he was, people went throughout that entire region gathering the sick and the afflicted and bringing them to him that they might be healed.

The episode of those lost hogs had doubtless been forgotten, at least overshadowed by the realization that here was that great and wonderful Physician who was able to heal humanity's ills.

Could not this healed demoniac have been responsible for bringing relief to so many who might otherwise have continued suffering because of the reaction of those disgruntled hog raisers (who, incidentally, were not Israelites)? And now they had opportunity to listen to Jesus' great message of eternal salvation.

He too is among the anonymous who can speak to us today and remind us of what is needed out there where needy people, and people who are not coming to our churches, will be able to see firsthand what God can do for them also, not only physically and economically but spiritually. Like these Gerasenes, they can and must be reached by us if they are to learn what Jesus has done for us and is able also to do for them.

This man can remind us that in addition to meeting and hearing the testimonies of others and giving our own testimony or perhaps merely remaining silent, we should be out there letting people know what salvation has meant to us and can mean to them. How else can they be reached? What a challenge this healed man is giving us!

Water Carrier

John 4:1-42

Returning from the city of Sychar, the disciples were amazed to find their Master talking with a woman—and a *Samaritan* woman, which in those days was not customary.

As if this were not a sufficient shock, when the woman had gone they offered Jesus food which they had walked into Sychar at noon to procure, but they were informed that he had already partaken of food of which they had no knowledge.

What did that mean? Surely the woman had not given it to him. Samaritans, who had no more dealings with Israelites than Israelites had with them, actually resented their passing through their territory, especially if they were going in the direction of Jerusalem.

If the disciples had known what Jesus knew about her reputation, (see vv. 17-18), their amazement would have been greater. John had no idea that one day he would be recording a full account of this very strange incident.

This was a tremendously important encounter, not merely for the woman herself, nor for her friends in Sychar, nor for the disciples, but for all future generations.

What motive did Jesus have for going through Samaria instead of bypassing it, as was the custom of the Israelites? Was it merely to drink water from the ancient well of Jacob? His motive was far greater and more important.

The disciples were to learn of a supply of food of which they had not known. This woman was to learn of a supply of living, inexhaustible water springing up within the heart—yes, and much more.

The manner in which the Lord Jesus conducts the conversation with this woman as he unfolds his wonderful truth is in itself a fascinating study and worthy of emulation, convincing her that she is actually speaking with a prophet.

When she becomes convinced of this, she voices a belief held by people of many ancient nations that their gods were limited in power to their own territorial borders, a belief voiced by the advisers of King Benhadad after his powerful military machine was defeated by the Israelites (1 Kings 20:23).

And later when the Syrians conquered Samaria, they took into captivity all but the poorest of the people, whom they replaced with captives from other nations, thus establishing a hybrid nation which adopted a hybrid religion.

The time is now at hand, Jesus informs her, when God would be worshiped, not only in one particular place as in Jerusalem or Samaria. Then he speaks these wonderful words:

"But an hour is coming, and is now, when the true worshipers

101

will worship him in spirit and truth, for the Father seeks such as worship him. God is (not a spirit, but) Spirit, and it is necessary for those worshiping him to worship him in spirit and truth" (John 4:23-24).

Leaving her water pots at the well, the woman returned to Sychar and told the men what Jesus had said to her. Going out to the well with her, they then believed not because of her testimony but because of their personal contact with the Son of God, the Source of this inexhaustible supply of living water.

This revolutionary truth which Jesus disclosed to the Samaritan woman is one which many have been slow or reluctant to comprehend. Many Israelites who confessed their faith in Jesus as their Savior, their promised Messiah, were stubbornly reluctant to share this good news with people of other nations. The efforts of the apostle Paul and others, who in obedience to the Great Commission of the Lord and the leadership of the Holy Spirit carried the gospel to people of other nations, were vigorously opposed by Israelites, who forced Paul and his co-workers to cross over and help the people of Macedonia and to move on and spread the gospel.

And so this woman is remembered not merely because Jesus asked her for a drink of water from Jacob's well but because Jesus opened that perpetual stream of living water which, though often polluted by obstinate, selfish, willful humans, is still available to all who will respond, as did she and the men following her out there to meet and hear Jesus.

Thus Jesus, not merely by word of mouth but by means of this wonderful example, was laying the groundwork for those not-too-distant days when he would commission his disciples to go out in like manner and contact people throughout the entire world.

The woman's name? We know her only as a Samaritan woman who was despised by Israelites but loved by the Son of God.

Inquiring Aliens

John 12:20-22   Sir, we desire to see Jesus.

Many were coming to see and hear Jesus, some from considerable distances. Then what was so unusual about the coming of these men wanting to see him?

These men were Greeks, and the Judeans were taught to be careful about having dealings with foreigners.

However, as these Greeks were in Jerusalem during the season of the Passover, we can be reasonably certain that these were devout proselytes who, having heard about Jesus and perhaps observed him at a distance and heard him speak, now wanted to meet him. Everyone about Jerusalem was talking about him.

Could it be that this was actually the promised Messiah?

But why did they not approach Jesus directly, instead of through his disciples? As they were aliens, could they not have been apprehensive lest the Messiah might react unfavorably to their desire to approach him directly?

What is more, they were coming at the time when the Pharisees and Sadducees engaged in their intensive effort to trap him and do away with him.

What was their reason for approaching Philip of Bethsaida? Was it because of his Greek name? Had they previously known or heard of him? Was he especially amiable or approachable? It was he who had informed Nathanael that he had found the Messiah and then introduced him to Jesus.

Then Philip informed Andrew. In consideration of their amazement at finding Jesus talking to that Samaritan woman at Jacob's well and their experience with that Syrophoenician woman who had insisted that Jesus go with her and heal her son, their hesitant attitude is quite understandable. Or were they perhaps apprehensive lest this might be another plot of the Jewish leaders?

Whether they actually brought the Greeks to Jesus or whether they merely informed him of their desire to see him, John does not tell us. Nor do we know how many Greeks there were.

However, the reaction of the disciples is actually overshadowed by the effect which this encounter had upon the Messiah himself. When Andrew passed this information to him, Jesus uttered these dramatic words:

"The hour has come, that the Son of man must be glorified" (v. 23).

His heart is touched to overflowing. The great event is now at hand, the agony of the cross and all that it is to mean is pressing in upon him.

He now speaks of a grain of wheat which, after being planted in the soil, must die before it can bear fruit; otherwise, it is left alone. And, after saying that one must lose one's life in order to gain it, once again he foretells his own death and prays that the name of God may be glorified. From heaven came this response:

"I have both glorified it, and shall glorify it again" (v. 28).

His soul is greatly troubled because of that awful experience which is now close at hand. And yet this is the purpose for which he had descended into the world.

Previously he had instructed his disciples to go only to the lost sheep of Israel (Matt. 10:5-6; 15:24). He had, however, informed them that there were also other sheep in which he was interested (John 10:16). He needed to go through Samaria, and soon he would commission them to begin there at Jerusalem and go out to all nations.

What has all this to do with the coming of these foreigners?

At hand was the fulfillment of that prophecy which his heavenly Father had made to Abraham long ago—that he would not only make of him a great nation but that through that nation he would reach out to *all* the nations.

This episode should keep alive in the minds of posterity this great truth that the Savior came to seek and to save people of all nations who, like these Greeks, would desire to see him, and that we are not the only ones for whom the Savior laid down his life.

One wonders whether, after the resurrection and the opportunity was given, these inquisitive Greeks again desired to see Jesus—this time because he had died and conquered death to save them. The disciples who heard these words were reluctant to share the good news with people of other nations.

Are we, like them, perplexed when strangers come expressing a desire to meet the Savior? Or do we introduce them to him?

Then Whose?

Matthew 22:23-33 [1] *. . . for they all had her.*

Although the Pharisees and Sadducees had little regard for each other, both parties were resorting to every possible means to bring the Lord Jesus into disfavor and disrepute with the people and, if possible, to find a means of doing away with him. They were unaware that in so doing they were actually aiding him in carrying out the objective for which he had descended into the world.

The Sadducees were not accusing this woman of breaking the law of Moses. On the contrary, they represented her as having actually fulfilled faithfully one of the statutes. [2]

The woman herself did not actually utter a word. As a matter of fact, she was not even present. What is more, she was not even living, if indeed she had ever lived. Scholars are of the opinion that this was probably a stock conundrum used by those Sadducees to bolster their contention that there would not be a resurrection.

In this instance the Sadducees were seeking to hold Jesus up to ridicule, by pointing out the predicament in which this poor woman would find herself *if* there were a resurrection; which of those seven brothers would be her husband there in heaven?

But what sort of message could be handed down to posterity by a woman who on that occasion did not utter a word, was not even present, was no longer alive—if, indeed, she had *ever* lived?

As on other occasions, Jesus gives them an answer which actually embarrasses and holds them up to ridicule, causing them to resort to other means of silencing and doing away with him.

That, he is telling them, is men's conception of heaven, not based upon what God has in store for those who choose to go there. Heaven is not on their own terms, but on God's terms, on his resourcefulness, ingenuity, and benevolence, which humans are too frequently prone to underestimate.

The Savior responds by asking *them* a question: "Isn't this the reason that you are in error, knowing neither the Scriptures nor the power of God?" (Mark 12:24).

Their question calls forth such counterquestions as these: In what respect would heaven differ from earth with all of its problems and relationships? Where would our self-satisfaction begin and theirs end and vice versa—especially when our individual interests would differ and clash?

That question involving this poor woman and her seven husbands presents no more of a distorted conception of heaven than many of the opinions held by people today, including many sincere Christians. An attempt to summarize those various theories would be merely time-consuming. In many instances they are expressions of self-enjoyment, self-indulgence, concern for a limited number of people, particularly their own family, their own circle of friends.

What of our relationship with God and his Son whose earthly ministry has made heaven available to us? What do we desire to build upon that sure foundation which Jesus has laid at so great a sacrifice? Do we build superstructures of our own choosing and making to our own glory or to *his?*

The apostle Paul has left us this challenging answer: "For no one is able to lay another foundation apart from the one having been laid, who is Christ Jesus" (1 Cor. 3:11). He then admonishes us to be very careful how we build; for whatever we build will be tested as by fire, and, as we know, fire either purifies or destroys.

The vitally important message which can be given to posterity by this woman, or one in similar circumstances, is something like this: "Don't be alarmed or misled by a case like mine. Look to the One who came to earth that you may have eternal life and have it more abundantly" (John 10:10).

Jesus has left us comparatively few details concerning heaven. But when considering the wonderful things which we are still learning about of this world and of its surroundings (which will one day pass away), why should we entertain limited, dubious views, doubts, or questions with reference to that wonderful place whither Jesus Christ has gone to prepare for us an abode to which he has promised to take us (John 14:1-3). "Otherwise (if this were not so) I would have told you," he adds.

All of this and more we can learn from the case of this woman, be she real or fictitious, who actually did not utter a word.

[1] See also Mark 12:18-27; Luke 20:27-40.
[2] Deuteronomy 25:5-10, a law also observed by Ruth.

Owners of a Colt

Matthew 21:1-11; Mark 11:1-11; Luke 19:29-44   Why are you untying the colt?

We know in whose tomb Jesus' body rested on the sabbath between his crucifixion and resurrection. But this colt on which he made his triumphal entry into Jerusalem—to whom did it belong?

Oh, well! why be bothered about a mere beast of burden and its owners? Of what significance could that be?

This was, as a matter of fact, by no means an unimportant event in the life of the Son of God. It did not signify, as many including his own disciples thought at the time, the prelude of the collapse of his earthly ministry.

It was in fact the prelude of that climactic event for which he had relinquished equality with his heavenly Father and descended into this world, as so graphically described by the apostle Paul in Philippians 2:5-8.

The Son of God did not intend to slip into Jerusalem like a vanquished hero, a most-wanted criminal or impostor, as those religious leaders considered him. The significance of this event is therefore as great as was his birth in a manger of the virgin Mary or his burial in that borrowed tomb belonging to Joseph of Arimathea.

Note also that Mark and Luke record that no one had previously ridden on this borrowed colt (Mark 11:2; Luke 19:30).

This animal could, as a matter of fact, be compared with a royal limousine of our era. The Son of God was riding at the head of this triumphal procession with both adults and children singing and spreading branches, even their own garments, on the road over which he was to travel. Those claiming to be the spiritual leaders of Israel raised their voices in angry protest.

When those leaders asked Jesus to tell the multitude to be still, he informed them that if they were to be still the very rocks would cry out, so vitally important was this event (Luke 19:39-40).

Jesus had been informing the disciples of what would await him in Jerusalem. This demonstration would actually add fuel to the efforts of his adversaries. Yet none of these circumstances could deter him from entering voluntarily into this sacred center of worship where for centuries offerings and sacrifices had been made to the living God and where now he, God's own Son, was about to offer himself, the eternally acceptable atonement for the sins, not only of the Israelites but of the entire world.

A matter of minor significance, this incident of a borrowed colt? Far from it! And now, as Jesus was ready to complete his mission of love and grace, here was an opportunity for someone to render a real service, merely by lending him a colt.

Who were the owners of this colt? There were more than one, we are informed.

Since they lived in the vicinity of Bethany, had they been out there when Jesus told Lazarus to come out of the tomb? Were they among the guests at the feast when one of Lazarus' sisters anointed the Lord for his burial?

Had they not been present, surely they would have heard spectacular reports. And were they now curious enough to follow in order to earn for what purpose the Lord needed their colt? Did it walk on *their* garments also?

As he had promised, surely Jesus saw to it that it was returned to its owners—it would of course have sufficient "horse sense" to find its way back home!

Though their inquiry as to why the disciples were untying the animal might raise a question in our minds, yet, when informed, they raised no objection, as Jesus had said. They therefore had some knowledge of the Lord Jesus and his great ministry.

The suggestion that the animal might have belonged to Lazarus would of course add interest to the event, but, had that been true, surely at least one of the Gospel writers would have recorded it.

We might add, ironically, that the colt has been given more attention or publicity than the colt's owners!

Could this be the message which those owners would send over the centuries? "How meaningful this could have been to us, but how little posterity knows about our reaction to this wonderful privilege that came our way, having so important a part in glorifying the Messiah! Don't fail to make use of the opportunities that come *your* way."

Malefactor

Luke 23:39-43

Both of the condemned criminals who were crucified on either side of Jesus joined the mob in reproaching Jesus (Matt. 27:44).

However, when one of them denounced the Lord for not relieving their intense suffering and delivering them from that horrible torture, his companion rebuked him:

"Don't you even fear God, seeing that you are under the same judgment; and we are receiving that which we deserve?" (Luke 23:39 ff.).

Then he said this: "Jesus, remember me whenever you come into your kingdom" (v. 42).

What was it that caused this man to change his attitude? Was it the wonderful manner in which the Savior was reacting under these trying circumstances, or was it the intensity of his own suffering. Perhaps, as he intimated to his fellow criminal, it was the sense of his own guilt induced by this torture and slow death?

Whatever the reason, we can be assured of his sincerity because of the Lord Jesus' response to his earnest petition.

Jesus did not reprimand him for his previous antagonistic attitude or because of his guilt, which he had acknowledged. Nor did he relieve him of his excruciating pain. Jesus stopped dying long enough to assure him: "I truly tell you, today you shall be with me in Paradise" (v. 43).

This repentant criminal's experience has been adopted as a pattern by many who, aware that they must ultimately surrender to God, have no intention of doing so until they are certain that they are near the end of life. They consider eternal salvation as nothing more than fire insurance designed to protect them from eternal punishment in hell.

They do not stop to consider, however, that this repentant robber might not previously have heard Jesus' message of eternal salvation by grace through repentance and faith in him. There is absolutely no foundation for such a presumptuous assumption that the repentant criminal had been guilty of procrastination, as do some who deliberately postpone so vitally important a decision until they think they are nearing death's door.

What assurance could they possibly have that they too will be given this same opportunity? The assurance that their death will not be sudden, unexpected, as is true in many instances?

What is more, living one's life in one's own way, unwilling to conform to the manner of life perscribed by God and this Son, Jesus, yet expecting to be permitted to slip into heaven and enjoy eternal life, is a deliberate affront to God the Creator, Sustainer, and Redeemer. This is a deliberate affront to Jesus who has made so great a sacrifice to make eternal life available to them with so little personal sacrifice on their part. Such a thoughtless, selfish attitude is not even worthy of intelligent human reasoning.

There is still another vitally important point to be made with reference to this wonderful experience, which might well be termed a deathbed confession. And surely this is the message which he could and would convey to the people of our day.

"Let me remind you that only 50 percent of those of us who died there beside the Savior that day received the assurance of being with the Lord in Paradise."

And he would add: "Too much is at stake for you to take that needless risk, as my buddy dying there on the other side of the Lord Jesus could remind you. It might mean forfeiting your own eternal salvation, this privilege of being with the Savior here in eternal Paradise."

Who was he? All that we actually know about him is that now he is where we are looking forward to being, with Jesus in Paradise, where no one or nothing can separate us from Christ Jesus, who died there that we might live with him.

Beggar's Bonanza

Acts 3:1 to 4:31   Silver and gold I do not have.

Day after day he was carried to the entrance of the Temple, to lie there waiting, begging, hoping, frustrated, disappointed, and wondering how and when it was going to end.

One day he attracted the attention of two men about to enter the Temple. When he asked them for alms, one of them fastened his gaze on him and said, "Look at us."

Surely he was going to receive something from them. Oh, what a letdown when one of them said: "Silver and gold I don't possess." Then why did the man stop and raise his hopes in that way? Why didn't he go inside and pray?

A great deal can flash through a human mind in a fleeting second; the imagination is not hindered by the lapse of time required to put one's thoughts into words. After that split second he heard:

"But what I have I'm going to give you."

What flashed through his mind during that next second? "Some more of that sympathy? Or perhaps more of that free advice which some people are always ready to hand out, people who have no idea what I endure day after day, just lying here waiting, hoping . . . ? Suppose *he* had to—

"What did he say? Did I understand him to tell me to get up and walk? He must be—"

By this time Peter had him by the hand and was pulling him to his feet. To his utter amazement, for the first time in his entire life he was able to stand up and walk!

"Oh, praise God! Praise Jehovah of hosts! I can walk!"

Unmindful of his surroundings and what people might think or say, he leaped about, shouting. The people came running to learn the meaning of all of this commotion. "What happened?"

When they recognized who the man was, they were amazed and were eager to learn: "How did such a miracle come about?"

Now the man who told him to stand up and walk is boldly informing that crowd of Israelites in no uncertain terms that the man

111

was healed by the power of "him whom you turned over to Pilate and denied . . . whom God raised up from the dead and we are witnesses."

This was the man who not very long ago had been afraid to admit to a maidservant that he even *knew* the Son of God!

And to think that all of this had come about because of what Peter was able to give this poor beggar who had been asking things from other people but now was doing something for them—helping Peter to preach this sermon—*as a living illustration!*

"Oh-oh! Here come those Temple guards. *And are they upset!* What do they want?"

They did not have long to wait for the answer. Peter, John, and this healed man identified only as a beggar, lame from birth, are arrested, being charged with peace disturbance and for giving the credit for this man's miraculous healing to the one whom they had delivered to the Roman authorities to be executed.

Now what was in store for this poor beggar? *More* trouble?

On the following morning a number of Jewish leaders were called together, and Peter, John, and the healed man were brought before them. Since those Jewish leaders were the ones who had demanded the death of him in whose name they had been proceeding, what hope was there now for *them?*

When asked by what authority they had acted on the previous day, under the direction of the Holy Spirit, Peter used this opportunity to inform them that it was in the name of him for whose death they, those who now sat in judgment over them, had been responsible, the risen Lord Jesus Christ.

Recognizing that these two plain, uneducated men had been with Jesus and seeing this invalid standing on his own feet before them, those dignitaries *had absolutely nothing to say!* They went into a private session and calling back the three ordered them never again to speak out "in that name." Then Peter, John, and the healed man were free.

But not before Peter and John said to them: "If it is the right thing in God's sight to listen to you rather than to God, you decide, for we are not able to keep quiet about what we have seen and heard" (Acts 4:19-20).

Being set free, they immediately went to the other followers of

112

Jesus and reported what had taken place, and they all rejoiced because of what the risen Lord had wrought through them!

They who had no silver or gold gave this invalid something far more valuable, which enabled all three to witness to those worshipers, to those Temple authorities, and to those Jewish leaders in the name of the Christ whom they had delivered to the Roman authorities to be killed.

What a challenge this healed beggar has for us. We are to share with others in this materialistic age not tangible things nor a mere wish that we could do something to help them but share the spiritual message of what the risen Savior has done for us and is able and more than willing to do for them.

Exorcists

Acts 19:11-19   Jesus I know, and . . . but you . . . ?

Does the name Sceva suggest anything to you?

All that we know about him is contained in verse 14. He was a Jewish high priest, and he had seven sons. Whether they were active members of the Sadducean party, as was their father, we are not informed. However, their conduct clearly indicates that they were not of the Sadducees and that they also were not followers of the Lord Jesus Christ.

They were among a group of Jewish exorcists who wandered into Ephesus, a city where idolatry and superstition were in abundance.

Observing the unusual miracles which God was performing through the apostle Paul in driving out evil spirits and healing, these seven decided that if this worked for Paul surely it ought to work for them also.

This, incidentally, would indicate that their own practice of sorcery was ineffective; otherwise why should they desire to change their tactics?

Their motive, of course, was different from that of Paul. They were not particularly interested in healing poor sufferers or in promoting the kingdom of God; they wanted to make that a part of their own hocus-pocus, and since the use of Jesus' name worked for the apostle Paul, *why shouldn't* it work for them?

113

And so they approached a man and called: "I adjure you in the name of Jesus whom Paul is proclaiming . . . "

Their hocus-pocus boomeranged! The evil spirit responded but not in the manner in which they had anticipated: "Jesus I know, and Paul I understand, but you, who are you?" (v. 15).

And leaping upon them, the man sent them away minus their attire and badly bruised!

Nevertheless, even though these seven unnamed sons of Sceva failed in their effort to rid that man of his malady, they are still in a position to do something to relieve people in our era. We are constantly hearing of new cults, sects, and movements which, when carefully scrutinized, prove not to be in harmony with the great plan of salvation by the grace of God through and in the name of his Son, Christ Jesus. Although not as disastrous as in the case of these seven in many if not all instances, they are not as effective as their practitioners would have people believe.

To justify such practices, the argument is sometimes used that "people are hungry for that sort of thing," healing, speaking in tongues, and the like, providing excitement and glamor.

The response is that there is ample spiritual nourishment and satisfaction and uplift for those who will reach out for it in the name of Christ Jesus, and in the manner in which he provided.

Merely because such punitive measures are not immediately administered to those engaging in similar practices today, it should not be interpreted as proof that they are exceptions, looking as if to be in harmony with the will and purpose of God and therefore meeting his divine approval.

In many instances the results are questionable or are entirely negative and, one might add, are harmful and misleading to both those participating and those who are sidetracked by their example.

God is not standing over us ready to pounce upon us, as was true in this instance. On the contrary, he instructs, challenges, and encourages us to utilize our intelligence for both his interest and our own interest in promoting his divine objectives.

Furthermore, Jesus has warned us as to the outcome of cases similar to this. People who will stand up before him in the judgment, saying: "Did we not do this or do that in your name!" will be informed: "Depart from me . . . I never knew you" (Matt. 7:23).

They too were working in their own interest, and not in his.

And it would be well to remind ourselves of something else which the Lord Jesus said, and which is applicable to cases of this nature: "They have their reward" (Matt. 6:2).

Why be misled by humanly inspired ideas, schemes, and practices when divinely orientated practices will be rewarded with positive and eternal results?

All of this and more is included in the message which these seven unnamed sons of that Judean priest could deliver, were they able to speak to us today.

Ethiopian Eunuch

Acts 8:26-40

Among those Christians who left Jerusalem because of the vigorous persecution of Saul of Tarsus was Philip, one of the seven who had been chosen by the church to those neglected Greek widows.

He went over to the city of Samaria, where he began preaching and performing miracles.

One day at noon, under instruction of a messenger of God, he started down the road through that desolate region between Jerusalem and Gaza. At the direction of the Holy Spirit he hopped up into a chariot, behind an Ethiopian eunuch.

He was a devout proselyte of Judaism, indicated by his reading— *aloud*—a passage from the prophecy of Isaiah. He was certainly a remarkable man of ability and trustworthy, as is evident from his position as Queen Candace's secretary of the treasury. That he was a remarkable man is revealed by his having taken time off to go to Jerusalem, undoubtedly to worship.

Philip's method of dealing with this man is in itself deserving of special attention; it was direct, tactful, effective.

"Do you understand what you are reading?" he began.

"How can I," was the man's response, "unless someone explains it to me? Of whom is the prophet writing, of himself or of someone else?"

What an opening for the evangelist! And by the time they came to a lake or stream of water, the man stopped the chariot. "Here's water. What's to hinder me from being baptized?"

When he had confessed his faith in the Lord Jesus Christ as his Savior, they went down into the water and Philip baptized him.

Coming up out the water, the Ethiopian glanced about but could not find Philip who had been whisked away by the Holy Spirit, and was on his way down to Caesarea, where years later he was found witnessing for the Lord Jesus—and by the man who was responsible for his leaving Jerusalem . . .

But what became of this remarkable Ethiopian proselyte to Judaism who was regenerated by the One of whom Isaiah had prophesied and who had gone one great step farther than many of those Judeans who had succeeded in proselyting him.

All that we can learn further from the Scriptures is that he continued on his homeward journey happily worshiping God.

However, it is unnecessary to draw very heavily upon our imagination in speculating about a man who, occupying so high a position in his government in the service of his queen, had taken time off to travel so far to worship the true God and had been redeemed through God's own Son, having been baptized immediately revealing his sincere conviction.

Surely one of his caliber would accomplish something worthwhile for his newly-found Savior, like his newly-found evangelistic friend. Although whatever he actually accomplished must remain a matter of speculation, surely this aggressive Ethiopian shared the wonderful message of Isaiah and of Philip with his own people, under the direction of the Holy Spirit who had directed Philip to contact him on that lonely road that noonday.

We can be sure of this—his aggressiveness and his responsiveness can still influence us and inspire us to accomplish something worthwhile for our risen Lord and Savior, Christ Jesus.

It would be well also to remind ourselves that opportunities from the Holy Spirit, such as this one which the Holy Spirit so unexpectedly opened for Philip, can and will prove more fruitful than some of those which we try to open for ourselves, demonstrating again the supreme wisdom and wonderful leadership which God has made available to those of us who trust in him and seek to serve him.

Dream Man

Acts 16:6-12

Wherever in Asia Paul and those with him endeavored to go, they were hindered not only by those Judaizers who followed them and stirred up trouble but now by the Holy Spirit, under whose leadership they had been moving.

Then went to Phrygia, passed by the region of Galatia, then endeavored to go to Bithynia. Then they went to Troas.

Now where should they go, and what should they do? Where did the Holy Spirit want them to go?

Then one night down there in Troas Paul had a dream. Before him there stood a man, beckoning: "Come over into Macedonia, help us" (v. 9).

Who was this man who beckoned to Paul in that dream? Scholars have been speculating as to his identity. One suggestion has been that he might have been Luke. This, however, is ruled out because this is one of those "we passages" in Acts which indicate that Luke himself, the author of Acts, was with Paul, Silas, and Timothy during this experience.

Had Paul recognized this man who appeared to him in this dream? Had he done so, would he not have disclosed the man's identity to the others? Since his identity has not been disclosed, well might this be an indication that the man represented the multitude of those living over there who needed their message of salvation.

On, well, what is to be gained by speculating as to the identity of a man who merely appeared in a dream, who might never have existed in real life?

Actually the answer to this question, which gives us the clue to his identity, is contained in his words: "Come over . . . and help *us,*" which, as has just been suggested, clearly identifies him as one of those who needed them.

This also indicates the reason for our taking the time to consider him.

Real or imaginary, he is actually standing between two different

117

regions, Asia Minor and Macedonia, between Asia Minor and Europe, East and West—and, as a matter of fact, between Asia Minor and the rest of the world, for which the Messiah came, lived and died, and with which he commanded his disciples to share this Good News.

Immediately "we"—Paul, Silas, Timothy, Luke, and whoever else was with him, concluded that this was the answer which they had been seeking. And so they went over into Macedonia and into Philippi where a splendid work was started and was carried on to Athens, Ephesus, Colossae, and other places. Ultimately Paul went as far as Rome, and if his intentions were fulfilled, he went even farther.

Frequently over these many centuries has this dream man's brief but profound plea reechoed, in one form or another. And how often has it echoed to people who have been satisfied and content to consider that the gospel was particularly for them, in turn failing or refusing to share the good news and thus help others in need of the Savior.

This dream man's plea can still be reechoed, even though his might have been only a visionary voice. Think of this in terms of our own situation.

Over and over, in one form or another, this dream man's plea keeps coming to our own land, to which during the past few centuries people came in search of a place where they could worship God without being molested by those who, as in Paul's day, would not permit them to serve and worship God in the manner in which they desired and felt that they should worship him.

Ironically, numbered among those foreign fields are places in which the gospel was proclaimed during the ministry of Paul and his fellow missionaries!

Could it be possible that if we should fail to respond to this dream man's plea, people in our own land may be in need of this man's plea, merely because we today are not listening as he calls from those foreign lands: "Come over and help us"?

Ventriloquist

Acts 16:13-24

After their arrival in Philippi, Paul and those with him went down to the riverbank on the sabbath in search of a prayer group. As there were few Israelites in Macedonia, there was no synagogue.

Finding a group of women, they sat down and talked with them. The Lord touched the heart of a dealer in purple from Thyatira named Lydia, with the result that she and her household, perhaps women in her employ, were baptized.

Then she persuaded them to be her guests.

And so they were making a very good beginning in Philippi— until a strange girl began following and pestering them. Day after day she followed them, calling people's attention to them.

Luke describes her as one having an evil spirit of divination, and that she was practicing ventriloquism.

It was not what the girl was saying that disturbed Paul and Silas. As a matter of fact, what she kept yelling was: "These men are servants of the most high God, who are proclaiming to you the way of salvation" (v. 17).

In time, however, that sort of publicity can become annoying, can in fact have an adverse effect upon people, particularly when it comes from the wrong source.

After enduring this as long as he was able, Paul turned and called: "I order you in the name of Jesus Christ to come out of her." And within the hour, Luke writes, the spirit left her.

This girl was a slave, who through her ventriloquism had been bringing in quite a bit of money for her masters. Realizing that their source of income had suddenly been cut off, they seized Paul and Silas, dragged them before the city authorities, and accused them of stirring up the people.

The authorities ordered Paul and Silas to be beaten publicly and committed to jail, with instructions that they be kept in maximum security. And the warden, receiving this instruction, fastened their feet in wooden stocks and confined them in an inner dungeon.

And so what had promised to be a wonderful beginning there in Philippi seemed suddenly to have collapsed. Was this what that man in Paul's dream had beckoned them to come over and help them do?

Nevertheless, even so great a catastrophe did not dishearten these two missionaries. Nor did they exercise their privilege as freeborn Roman citizens to obtain their release from prison where they had been confined without a trial—even though Paul would do so the following day when the authorities sent word that they were to be released (v. 35).

That same night—and at midnight despite their bleeding backs—they were praying to God and singing!

And what is more, out of that prayer meeting out there on the riverbank and that visit to the home of Lydia was to grow one of the most fruitful churches which God through Paul established.

This slave girl who was instrumental in their being treated in that manner, what became of her? Did she become a member of that Philippian church? What a wonderful testimony she could have given no longer under the influence of that evil spirit, but under the direction and inspiration of the Spirit of God. What a testimony out of her own personal experience, bringing glory to God instead of financial gain to those who had held her captive!

Or now cast off and set adrift because she was no longer of any value to her owners, did she merely fade into obscurity? If so, what a negative message she could convey to many of our present era who, having received so much from God, reveal so little gratitude and go on as if nothing had taken place in their lives?

Who was this girl? There is nothing in the Scriptures to help us to identify her. And so the case must be closed with this old, familiar conclusion: "Identity Unknown."

Did *nothing* worthwhile result from the case, from the confinement of Paul and Silas in that dungeon? But that is another story!

Worried Warden

Acts 16:22-40   He was about to commit suicide.

Roused from sleep at midnight, the warden found the doors of the prison wide open. Surely the prisoners had escaped.

He was particularly concerned because of those two whom he had been ordered to keep in solitary confinement; they surely must have escaped. He drew his sword but not with the intention of going after them; he was about to take his own life, realizing that he would be held accountable for those two.

Out of the darkness he heard a voice. "Don't do yourself any harm; we're all here."

That he must see! Calling for a light, he "hoofed it in." [1]

Whether out of amazement or respect or reverence, we are not informed, but the warden fell at the feet of Paul and Silas—feet which earlier that day he had fastened in wooden stocks, in order to be doubly sure that they would not escape.

Had he been listening to their singing and praying and himself had peacefully fallen asleep with the assurance that everything would be all right?

After regaining his self-control, he inquired, "Gentlemen,[2] what must I do to be saved?" to which they answered:

"Put your trust (faith) in the Lord Jesus and you shall be saved . . ." (v. 31).

There followed one of the most amazing, unpremeditated, unprogrammed evangelistic campaigns recorded in Christian history. At that midnight hour the warden awakened his family, and they listened as Paul and Silas expounded the Word of God.

And as a result of this amazing midnight service, after washing their bloody backs, bruised by that flogging received on the previous day, the warden and his entire household were baptized.

And still that is not all. Taking them up into his own house, at that early morning hour, he set the table and they had a love feast; he and his family had confessed their faith in the Lord Jesus Christ.

Is it then any wonder that there in Philippi, with two remarkable

Christians, Lydia and this prison warden, there was established a church which became one of the most, if not *the* most beloved and esteemed churches which the apostle Paul had any part in establishing?

Who was this remarkable jailer? Would it not be interesting to be able to identify him by name? However, we must wait for that privilege until we, like him and his family, cross over into the Promised Land.

[1] This colloquialism is an accurate translation of the original Greek (v. 29). (See also Acts 14:14.)

[2] Greek *kurioi,* a polite term of address, like our word *gentlemen,* or the currently used *sirs.*

Harvesttime

Matthew 13:24-30,36-40

After this farmer had planted wheat in his field, an enemy slipped in one night and sowed darnel,[1] a bearded weed resembling wheat whose grain, when ripe, was black and unfit for any practical use.

When his servants discovered this, they came and asked whether they should dig up the darnel. If they did, was his response, they might also uproot some of the wheat.

"Let them grow until the time of harvest," he told them, "then separate them from the wheat, bundle them up, and burn them."

What is the interpretation of this illustration? This question was asked later by the disciples, and Jesus gave them a detailed explanation, setting forth truths as vitally significant today as when he spoke them, involving questions and arguments which are still raised by some of our contemporaries—but overlooked or disregarded by too many others.

"I'm just as good as some of your church members," is occasionally heard, either in self-defense or in self-justification.

There is in many instances an element of truth in this. As it was a bit difficult to distinguish between the growing wheat and darnel, it is often difficult to discern the difference between many professing Christians and non-Christians.

However, those who make this claim do not realize that the final test will not come until their earthly life is ended. When the grain was ready to be harvested, the darnel grains were black and, being unfit for any practical purpose, were bundled up and burned.

We of course know that grain does not harvest itself. Nevertheless, many humans have the idea that at the end of their lives they are going to be able to determine their own destiny, regardless of the manner of life they have lived.

No matter how nearly the human darnel may profess or appear to resemble the wheat of the kingdom of God, the final decision is going to be made by the Great Harvester. And although it is true that you can't fool all of the people all of the time, it should be remembered that you can't fool God *any of the time.* Here Jesus has assured us that only the human wheat is going to be retained.

It should be remembered that God does not look upon the outward appearance, but on the heart (1 Sam. 16:7).

The marvelous, miraculous truth involved here is that the Lord of the harvest has taken our place. In the terminology of this parable he *has actually burned in our place* that those of us who choose to do what it was impossible for the darnel to do may be completely transformed by that wonderful process of regeneration. This is only possible if we look to him for mercy and forgiveness before the time of harvest when the human darnel will be destroyed as by fire, along with the enemy who sowed it.

The question has also been raised: "Since this is true, why does the Great Harvester permit the wheat to continue growing along with the darnel? Why doesn't he uproot the darnel now, or transplant the wheat?"

The farmer himself has given us one of the several answers to this question. Life is so complex that none of us live entirely to ourselves and apart from others (Rom. 14:7).

Nor should we forget, contact with others can bring out the best that is within us, as well as purging the worst, depending upon the manner and degree in which we yield our lives to God and follow the teaching and the example of our Savior, the Lord Jesus Christ.

God has endowed us humans with the capacity to do our own thinking, make our own decisions, and carry them out or, in the language of this parable, actually have the opportunity of being transformed from darnel into wheat.

In addition, we who have already been transformed now have the opportunity and the privilege of persuading others to follow our example and do likewise.

Whether or not the Lord Jesus had a particular farmer in mind—doubtless many farmers have had similar experiences—it is of far greater importance that he has used this man to represent God himself, who has sent into this world his own Son to sow the seed, also sent his Holy Spirit to transform and nourish the plants in preparation for that great harvest.

It should be emphasized, however, that the One who is able and willing to change the nature of human plants has given this warning that he will *not* do so after our life on earth is over, nor *at or after the time of that great harvest.*

[1] Not tares.

Who Wrote This?

Hebrews 11:4   Having died, yet speaks.

Were we able to come up with the answer to this question, not only would our own curiosity be satisfied but one of the mysteries of the Scriptures would be solved.

"They from Italy greet you" (13:24).

This is the only personal message or greeting in the entire letter to the Hebrews.

If this appears to be a trivial matter, it should be pointed out that more is involved than may at first be realized. Conditions in the world today make this more significant to us.

If the epistle was sent from Italy, particularly if sent from Rome, there would be strong reason for the author to remain anonymous, due to the fact that the Christians were persecuted and driven out of Italy or compelled to go underground, taking refuge in the catacombs (see Acts 18:2).

Because at that time the Romans were in control of that entire part of the world, active Christians would be faced with the great and grave danger of being apprehended, particularly because of the antagonism of the Judaizers.

From these few words of greeting we are able to draw only negative conclusions. We are not informed who "they" were. Nor do we learn whether they had *sent* this epistle from Italy or whether they themselves had *gone* from Italy.

The author reveals a wonderful knowledge and training in Jewish history and practice; this is evident through the entire epistle. And this has led a few scholars to ascribe it to the apostle Paul.

Inasmuch, however, as thirteen of the Epistles were written or dictated and signed by him, this theory is hardly acceptable—unless he had a definite reason (for instance his unpopularity with the Judaizers). Yet Paul never hesitated to confront his own people with the gospel, even in the face of the danger of losing his life, for example, in Jerusalem before he appealed to Caesar (see Acts 21 ff.)

His imprisonment in Rome did not hinder him from sending several epistles bearing his name or from witnessing to those who visited him in prison while he was chained to Roman guards.

Could it have been written by John Mark, author of the gospel bearing his name, out of his Jewish background and his intimate contact with the Lord Jesus and his disciples?

The style of Hebrews has caused several scholars to suggest that it could be the work of Apollos, who before he was tutored by Aquilla and Priscilla had known only the teaching of John the Baptist.

Could it be the work of Priscilla herself, her anonymity being necessitated by the status of women in those times?

Another theory is that it might have been written by Barnabas, who, after he and Paul separated because of their disagreement over taking John Mark on their second missionary journey, faded into obscurity so far as we can learn from the book of Acts.

Whoever the author was, he or she has endowed us with a priceless heritage, clarifying the transition from Judaism to the fulfillment in the life, ministry, death, resurrection, and ascension into heaven of the Promised Messiah.

To what better source could one turn than to this wonderful letter to the Hebrews?

Hebrews contains a number of oft-quoted gems, such as the opening verses of chapter 11, the roll call of faithful saints who, having run their course so faithfully, have taken their places in heaven's grand-stand to cheer those who have replaced them in this great Christian struggle, encouraging us to remain faithful to the Author and Finisher of our faith, the Lord Jesus Christ, God's promised Messiah.

This unidentifiable author of Hebrews has become one of those who have joined the faithful who can encourage us to press on by faith in and through the Lord Jesus Christ.

The author has bequeathed something else upon us, which should not be overlooked or passed over lightly, that the value or importance of one's contribution to posterity need not be measured in terms of that individual's notoriety or popularity but rather in terms of the value of that individual's contribution itself.

Who we are may soon be forgotten or perhaps remembered dimly. What we may have contributed may be remembered; how long it will be remembered depends upon its worthwhileness. And if our contribution *is* worthwhile, it can benefit posterity much more than the remembrance of our identity.

The author of Hebrews has left us this monumental spiritual work of art without taking credit for it and for whatever contribution it has made and is still making to the lives of those who read it.